McGRAW-HILL

Language Arts

Vocabulary and Thesaurus

Workbook

Grade 5

McGraw-Hill School Division
New York • Farmington

McGraw-Hill School Division
A Division of The McGraw-Hill Companies

McGraw-Hill School Division
Two Penn Plaza
New York, New York 10121

Printed in the United States of America

ISBN 0-02-244785-7/5
5 6 7 8 9 021 05 04 03 02

TABLE OF CONTENTS

Vocabulary: Synonyms and Antonyms

Time-order words tell when events happen and in what order. Sometimes a phrase can show time order.

*One group of children began their camping trip **yesterday**. **In the meantime,** another group of children are enjoying a summer computer class.*

A. Read each sentence and find the time-order word or phrase. Write it on the line.

1. Before anyone set up a tent, the ranger explained the park's camping rules.

____

2. Parents of the campers had camped in this park a long time ago.

____

3. Some campers prepared dinner as soon as the tents were up.

____

4. Meanwhile, other campers gathered twigs and logs for the campfire.

____

5. Either today or tomorrow, everyone will enjoy a mountain hike.

____

Go on

B. Complete the paragraphs. Write the time-order word or phrase that best completes each sentence. Use each word once. Use capital letters when needed.

now	first	last night	tomorrow	next

6.-10. I need to write an essay about a surprising experience ________________. I can't write it ________________ because the assignment would be late. I couldn't write it ________________ because I had softball practice at 7:00 P. M. What I will write ________________ for the essay is my name and the date. ________________ I'll make up a good title to help with ideas.

finally	then	today	as soon as	after

11.-15. ________________ we went on a field trip. ________________ everyone assembled in the front hall, we were assigned seats. ________________ each student got on a bus as his or her name was called. ________________, we left for the theater. ________________ the bus pulled away, everyone talked about the play we were going to see.

Writing Activity

Write a paragraph that describes a class field trip--one that is made up or one that really took place. Use time-order words and phrases to show when events happened and in what order.

Idioms

Some words communicate ideas that do not match their dictionary meanings. These words or expressions are called **idioms**. For example, the idiom *let's call it a day* means, "let's consider our activity or work over with for now." Idioms are listed in the dictionary under the most important word in the phrase.

Read these sentences with idioms.

Time flies *whenever we're having fun.*

Clap ***in time*** *to the music.*

A. Write the answer to the questions.

1. Which word would you use to find the meanings of the idioms in the sample sentences? ____

2. In your own words, what does the idiom *time flies* mean?

____

____

3. Does *in time* mean "promptly" or "keeping the set rhythm" in the sentence above? ____

4. Rewrite the first sample sentence using the same ideas but without using an idiom.____

____

5. Use *in time* in your own sentence.

____

____

Go on

B. Underline the idiom in each sentence. Then write the meaning of the idiom in your own words.

6. If you don't enjoy volleyball, go fly a kite.

____

7. He let the cat out of the bag about the surprise party.

____

8. Drop me a line during your travels.

____

9. We're all in the same boat when it comes to sports.

____

10. I asked the other team to stop bugging me!

____

11. Were you pulling my leg when you said we would go to Spain?

____

12. Another win would be out of this world!

____

13. Hiking in the mountains is out of sight!

____

14. If I don't complete the practice, I'll be in hot water.

____

15. My dad plays the game by the book.

____

Writing Activity

Write a journal entry about vacation time or travel. Use at least three idioms. Read your journal entry aloud. Have classmates identify all the idioms you used.

Name ______________________ Date ______________ **VOCABULARY**

What Time Is It?

The answer to each riddle is a time-order word or phrase. Read the clue and write the answer on the line below each riddle.

today	last	now	second	tomorrow
yesterday	next	before	first	in the meantime

1. What word is a base in baseball and is before anything else?

____

2. What makes honey, lives in a hive, plus is the product of two times two ?

____

3. What word is used to call the marble at the end of a row and one piece of cake left on a plate?

____

4. What word is used to support an idea, back up a friend, or clock the winner of a race?

____

5. Which three words does a storyteller use to mean *while*?

____

6. What is something you don't do first, don't do third, and sounds like a nest in which eggs are placed just before the last consonant?

____

7. What is a twenty-four hour period of time that follows the opposite of "no" and the last syllable of another time-order word?

____

8. What is the word for a day for which the synonyms for each syllable are *also* + *extra* + *my goodness*!

____

9. What is a word that rhymes with the name of an animal that jumped over the moon and rhymes with what you say when something hurts?

____

10. What word could mean the double of a twenty-four hour period, another twenty-four hour period, and has two syllables?

____

Time Search

Look across and down to search for time-order words or phrases in the puzzle. Circle those you find. Then write the time-order words and phrases you find on the lines below.

I	N	C	O	N	C	L	U	S	I	O	N
T	A	S	F	O	L	L	O	W	I	N	G
U	N	O	I	P	A	Y	C	E	I	O	U
W	L	O	R	B	S	J	A	K	O	T	N
L	A	N	S	I	T	H	E	N	U	R	M
O	T	E	T	A	L	O	N	E	D	A	Y
X	E	R	I	O	Y	D	U	R	I	N	G
P	R	I	M	A	R	Y	A	L	Y	E	A

Words Across

1. ______________________

2. ______________________

3. ______________________

4. ______________________

5. ______________________

6. ______________________

Words Down

7. ______________________

8. ______________________

9. ______________________

10. ______________________

Name ______________________ Date ______________ **VOCABULARY**

Using a Dictionary

A dictionary can help you learn the meaning, spelling, and pronunciation of an unfamiliar word. The **entry** words are arranged in alphabetical order.

At the top of each page in the dictionary are two **guide words**. The first guide word is the first entry word on that page. The second word is the last entry word on that page.

opposition/orchard

opposition (op′ə zish′ən) **1.** act of opposing or the condition of being opposed; contrast. *Your answer is in opposition to the correct one.* **2.** fighting against or resisting: *Our plan met with great opposition.* **3.** anything that opposes; especially related to politics: *The opposition pledges to create new laws for the environment. noun*

A. Write the answer to the questions.

1. What is the first word that appears on this dictionary page?

____

2. What is the last word that appears on this dictionary page?

____

3. Would you find the word *oppose* on this sample page? Explain.

____

4. How many meanings does the word *opposition* have?

____

5. What do the sentences in *italic* print in this dictionary sample show you?

____

Go on

Name ______________________ Date ______________ **VOCABULARY**

B. List the words below under the correct dictionary page in alphabetical order. Use the guide words. If words begin with the same letter, look at the second letter. If the first two letters are the same, look at the third letter, and so on.

fission	dash	measure	crevice	duffel
ferret	nasal	fishery	mother	dungeon
creature	fault	morning	feature	napkin

crate/during

6. ______________________
7. ______________________
8. ______________________
9. ______________________
10. ______________________

farther/fossil

11. ______________________
12. ______________________
13. ______________________
14. ______________________
15. ______________________

meanwhile/nation

16. ______________________
17. ______________________
18. ______________________
19. ______________________
20. ______________________

Using a Thesaurus

A **thesaurus** is a reference source that lists synonyms for many common words. Synonyms are words that have the same or similar meanings. A thesaurus sometimes shows example sentences for the entry words and synonyms.

first *adj.* In time, before all others. *Please take the first right after you pass the library.*
adv. before anything or anyone else. *If you go first, I will follow you.*
▷ **initial** of or at the beginning. *The initial questions were easier than those at the end of the test.*
▷ **leading** out in front or guiding. *The leading horse found a good dirt path.*
▷ **primary** first in time order. *Our primary goal is to enjoy ourselves.*

A. Write the answers to the following questions.

1. In the thesaurus sample on this page, which is the entry word?

____

2. What is the meaning of *first*?

____

3. What do the words *initial*, *leading*, and *primary* have in common?

____

4. What is the purpose of the following sentence in the thesaurus sample above: *Please take the first right after you pass the library*?

____

5. Write a sentence using one of the synonyms for *first*.

____

Go on

B. Help Shawna revise this draft by finding new time-order words or phrases for each repeated and underlined word or phrase. Use the example sentences in the thesaurus in this book to make each paragraph better.

Arthur is my younger brother. Before he was born, I had one sister. **(6)** Before, I was the youngest in my family. **(7)** Before, my sister Angie was the only child. Now I am not the youngest child in my family. **(8)** Now I am the middle child.

After Arthur was born, my life changed. **(9)** After Arthur's arrival in our house, I moved out from my small bedroom. What did I do then? **(10)** Then I moved into a larger room. **(11)** Then I arranged things in the room. Meanwhile, little Arthur liked to sleep in the crib in my old room. **(12)** Meanwhile, Arthur squealed and cried if he wasn't asleep. During the night, Arthur was not my favorite family member. **(13)** During this time, my parents had their work set up at home.

(14) Now we all get along great! Now we are all five years older. Finally Angie and I are best friends. **(15)** Finally Arthur is old enough to have fun playing with us.

6. ______________________
7. ______________________
8. ______________________
9. ______________________
10. ______________________
11. ______________________
12. ______________________
13. ______________________
14. ______________________
15. ______________________

Vocabulary: Compound Words

A **compound word** is a word made from two or more words that have been joined together.

It snowed outside as we sat by the fireplace.
(compound as one word: *fire + place = fireplace*)

The fans cheered wildly during the play offs.
(compound as two words)

At the drive-in, we ordered lunch from the car.
(compound as two words joined by a hyphen)

A. Underline the compound word in each sentence. Then write the two words that make up the compound on the line.

1. The candidate gave handouts to voters.

____

2. Rashad's great-uncle had been mayor of the city.

____

3. This candidate wanted to help all the taxpayers.

____

4. She said, "Campaigns are like rides on a merry-go-round."

____

5. She promised a hit parade of laws to protect the environment.

____

Go on

B. To make a compound word, draw a line from a word on the left to a word on the right. Then write the compound word on the line. Check the spelling of the compound words in a dictionary.

6. count	**a.** grandmother	______________
7. home	**b.** president	______________
8. great	**c.** standing	______________
9. out	**d.** down	______________
10. vice	**e.** run	______________

C. Now write a sentence using each of the compound words you created in **B**.

11. ____

____

12. ____

____

13. ____

____

14. ____

____

15. ____

____

Writing Activity

Write the first paragraph for a speech about what you would do if you were elected as the first middle-school advisor to the vice-president of the United States. Use compound words.

Language History

> The English language grows and changes over time. Some words, especially compound words, are created to name new inventions or ideas. For example, a compound word such as *airplane* did not exist before the words *air* and *plane* existed. The word *airplane* was created to name the idea and invention of an airplane.
>
> *air* means "mixture of gases that surround the planet earth"
> *plane* means "flat, level, even"
> *airplane* means "flat structure, or plane, that flies through air"

A. Write the answer to the questions. Use a dictionary or a thesaurus to help you.

1. What are the two separate words that make up the compound word *spaceship*?

____

2. What is a spaceship?

____

____

3. Which meaning of *space* is used in *spaceship*?

____

____

4. Which meaning of *ship* is used in *spaceship*?

____

____

5. Why is *spaceship* a newer English word than either *space* or *ship*?

____

____

Go on

B. Write a definition for each compound word. Then write the definitions for the words that are used to form each compound word. Refer to a dictionary if you need to.

6. basketball: ______________________

____

basket: ______________________

ball: ______________________

7. film star: ______________________

film: ______________________

star: ______________________

____

8. hot dog: ______________________

hot: ______________________

dog: ______________________

____

9. software: ______________________

soft: ______________________

ware: ______________________

10. network: ______________________

net: ______________________

____

work: ______________________

Writing Activity

Write a paragraph that tells about how computers are used for communication. Use compound words. Then read your paragraph to a group of classmates, and explain the language history of each compound word.

Compound Scramble

Look at each group of four words. Combine the words to create a humorous phrase of two compound words. Write the phrase on the line.

1. hot away dog run ______________________

2. up walk moon town ______________________

3. pour sand down quick ______________________

4. snake left over rattle ______________________

5. water free melon throw ______________________

6. president drop vice rain ______________________

7. watch matter fact of wrist ______________________

8. bear gown grizzly night ______________________

9. stock topsy exchange turvy ______________________

10. elect foot bare president ______________________

11. sea cup tea weed ______________________

12. corn ear flower ring ______________________

13. board stick lip black ______________________

14. sauce in cave apple ______________________

15. happy people lucky go towns ______________________

Compound Circle

Write the answer to each clue in the appropriate "arm" of the circle. The answer to each clue is a compound word.

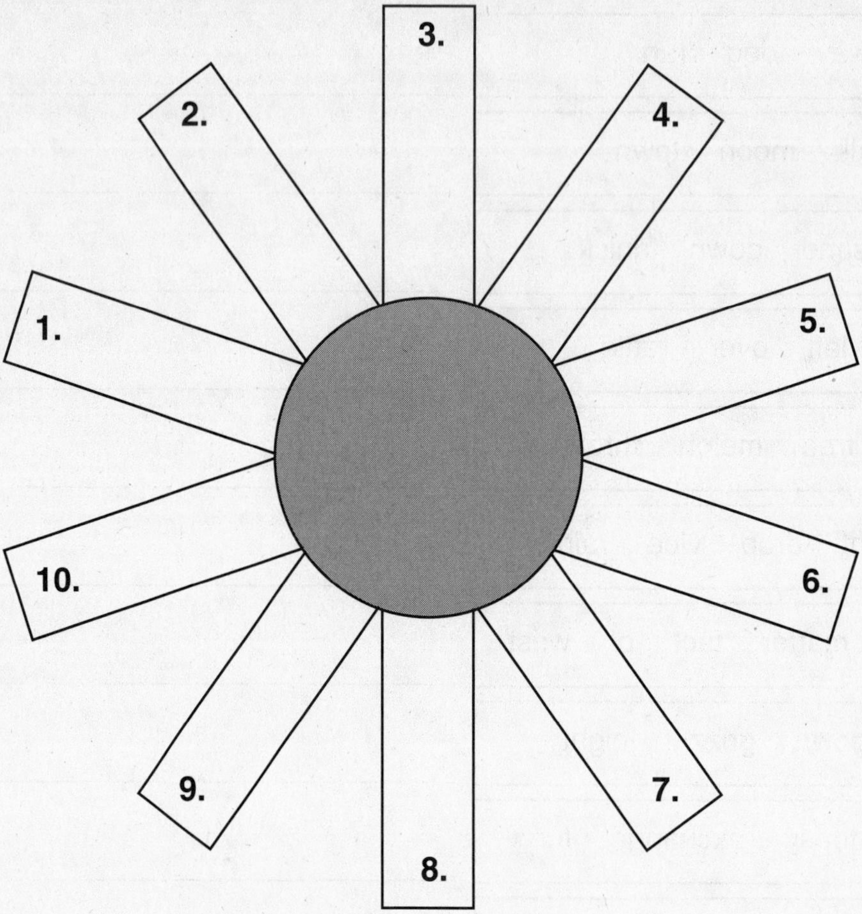

Clues

1. something you wear to protect eyes from the sun
2. a large yellow flower with seeds people like to eat
3. a day of the week that is also a homophone for a kind of dessert
4. what happens just before the sky becomes dark at night
5. a kind of roof or terrace that receives outdoor light
6. Egyptians and other ancient people worship this god of light.
7. This happens to introduce the morning.
8. a natural ray of light
9. a protective outdoor covering for skin
10. an instrument that shows time by measuring shadows and light

Circle the common word that appears in each compound word.

Using a Dictionary

You can use a **dictionary** to check the spelling of compound words. For example, the dictionary will show you if a compound word is written as one word, two separate words, or two or more separate words joined by a hyphen(s).

headlong/health

headlong (hed′lông′) **1.** With the head first.
2. In a hasty, careless way. *adverb*
Made with the head first. *adjective*

A. Write the answers to the questions.

1. What two words make up the compound *headlong*?

____

2. How many meanings are there for *headlong*?

____

3. Can *headlong* be used as a noun?

____

4. How is *headlong* used in this sentence: *She made a headlong dive into the pool*?

____

5. Write your own sentence using *headlong*.

____

____

Go on

B. Find the compound word in each sentence. Check the spelling in a dictionary and write the word with its correct spelling. Then tell how the word is used in the sentence by writing the part of speech.

6. Have you ever flown on an air craft?

____

7. Once, we flew on a very worth-while mission.

____

8. The secretary treasurer of a world organization led the mission.

____

9. Our goal was to make head way with endangered animals.

____

10. We took a ride into the wild to see grownup rhinos.

____

11. The loss of these great animals is just heart-breaking.

____

12. Some out standing people work to save rhinos.

____

13. Some of us master-minded a rally to save the rhinos.

____

14. At home, I became master-of-ceremonies for the rally.

____

15. We presented a lifesize picture of one of the rhinos we saw in the wild.

____

Using a Thesaurus

You have learned that a **thesaurus** is a reference source that provides synonyms—and sometimes antonyms—for many common words. Synonyms are words that mean the same or almost the same thing. Antonyms are words that have opposite meanings

A thesaurus also shows the part of speech for each entry word. This helps you learn how to use the word when you speak or write.

outstanding *adj.* stands out
▷ **distinguished** famous, stands out
▷ **famous** well-known, much talked about
▷ **notable** worth noticing or paying attention to
ANTONYM **ordinary**

A. Write the answers to the following questions.

1. What part of speech is *outstanding*?

____

2. What is the entry word in the thesaurus sample?

____

3. Which word would work best in a sentence that tells about "paying attention to"?

____

4. How does the word *distinguished* relate to the word *outstanding*?

____

5. What word could you use to mean the opposite of *outstanding*?

____

Go on

B. Read each sentence. Use the thesaurus in this book to replace each underlined word with a synonym that is also a compound word.

6. Only a few miles of road separate the towns.

____

7. What is something special you can do for your family?

____

8. Did you create the recycling club?

____

9. Lack of understanding made her feel concerned.

____

10. Helping someone gives you a rare feeling of accomplishment.

____

11. The play was good, but the ending made people feel sad.

____

12. People make better impressions when they are neat.

____

13. The figure in the painting is beautiful.

____

14. How many pupils have you talked with?

____

15. Can you identify where the meeting took place?

____

Vocabulary: Prefixes and Suffixes

A **prefix** is a word part added to the beginning of a root or a base word.
A **suffix** is a word part added to the end of a root or a base word.
Prefixes and suffixes change the meaning of the word to which they are added.

The shooting star was unbelievable.
(*un* + *believe* + *able* = unbelievable)
The prefix *un-* means "not."
The suffix *able* means "capable of."
So, *unbelievable* means "not capable of being believed."

A. Write the prefix or suffix in each underlined word. Then write the meaning of the word. Use a dictionary for help.

1. I would like to <u>relive</u> the day of the contest.

____

2. To my <u>amazement</u>, I won the trophy.

____

3. I sang as a <u>finalist</u> in an amateur contest.

____

4. My friends did not <u>foresee</u> this win.

____

5. Dad <u>replays</u> the video every week.

____

Go on

B. Join the prefix or base word on the right with a base word or suffix on the left to create a new word. Write the new word on the line.

6. bi	**a.** less	______________
7. worth	**b.** ist	______________
8. dis	**c.** ment	______________
9. punish	**d.** honest	______________
10. art	**e.** cycle	______________

C. Add a prefix or suffix to the underlined word to create a new word that makes sense in the sentence. Write the word on the line.

11. Do not <u>lead</u> me. ______________

12. How did you <u>act</u>? ______________

13. She is <u>able</u> to be here. ______________

14. This is a <u>play</u> space. ______________

15. Was the alarm set for <u>dawn</u>? ______________

Writing Activity

Use your imagination! Write an explanation of something incredible that happens in a dream. Use words with prefixes and/or suffixes.

Roots and Origins

Just as you can know people from other countries and cultures, you can get to know some of the words they use. Over time, some words from foreign languages have become familiar to people who use English. These words often appear in English fiction and nonfiction writing.

moccasin (Native North American)
chocolate (Native Mexican American)
hurricane (Native West Indian)
jaguar (Native South American)
et cetera (Latin)
bon voyage (French)
pasta (Italian)
taco (Spanish)

A. Write the answers. Use a dictionary if you need help.

1. A slipper made of soft leather is a

______________________________________.

2. A wild cat that runs very fast is a

______________________________________.

3. An expression that means “and others; so forth” is

______________________________________.

4. A food made from wheat in many shapes is

______________________________________.

5. A type of severe rainstorm is a

______________________________________.

Go on

B. Writers use words from other languages for accuracy in their descriptions. Write a sentence using each English word that originally comes from another language.

6. *Coyote* is Native Mexican American for "a small wolf-like animal."

____

7. *cul-de-sac* is a French word for "dead end."

____

8. *Eureka* is a Latin word for "I have found it."

____

9. *Barbecue* is Native West Indian for "meat roasted on an open fire."

____

10. *Spaghetti* is a type of pasta, an Italian food made from wheat.

____

Writing Activity

Write a short adventure story in which you use some words that originally came to English from other languages. Read your story to the class and challenge classmates to identify words that come from other languages.

Snake Roots

Snake your way down the page. On the line, write the word that fits each definition. Then identify the word root. Write the root in each numbered space. You can check word definitions and spellings in the dictionary.

ver = truth	soph = wise
sci = know	vinc = conquer
graph = write	luna- = moon
mech = machine	tract = drag
rupt = break	strict = pull

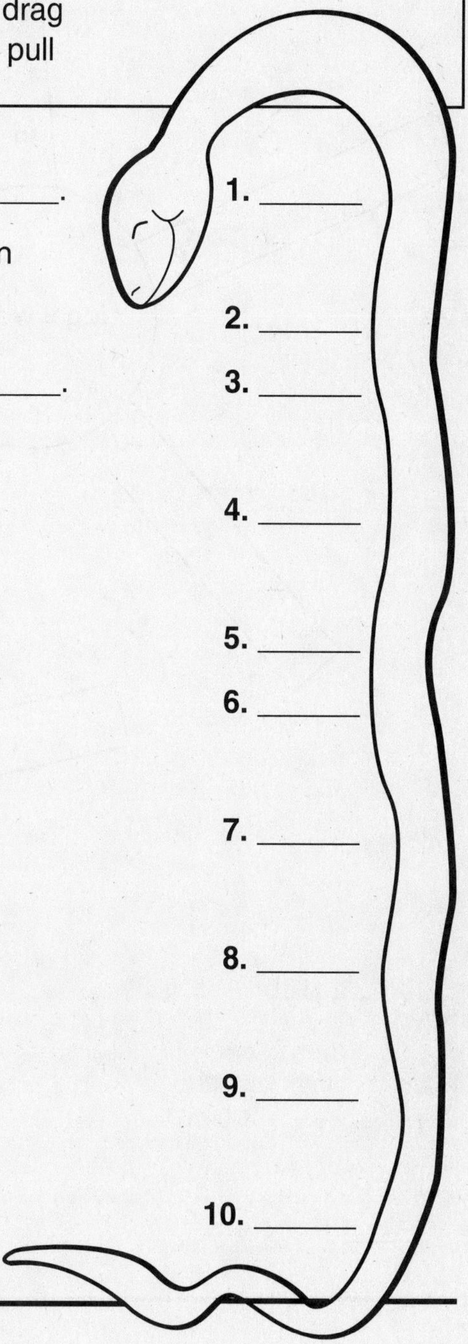

1. A handwritten name is called an ________________. **1.** ______

2. The person who works or fixes machines is known as a ________________. **2.** ______

3. This eclipse of the moon is called ________________. **3.** ______

4. The subject in school in which you might perform experiments is________________. **4.** ______

5. The decision reached by the jury in a trial is called a ________________. **5.** ______

6. An active volcano can ____________________. **6.** ______

7. The name for a student in the second year of high school is a ________________. **7.** ______

8. A math operation that uses the minus sign is called ________________. **8.** ______

9. When you win over people and they believe you, you ____________________ them. **9.** ______

10. Someone who makes you follow every rule is ____________________. **10.** ______

Sun Roots

At the center of each sun, you will find a Latin or Greek root that appears in many English words. On each ray of the sun, write an English word that includes that root. Use a dictionary or thesaurus to help you find words.

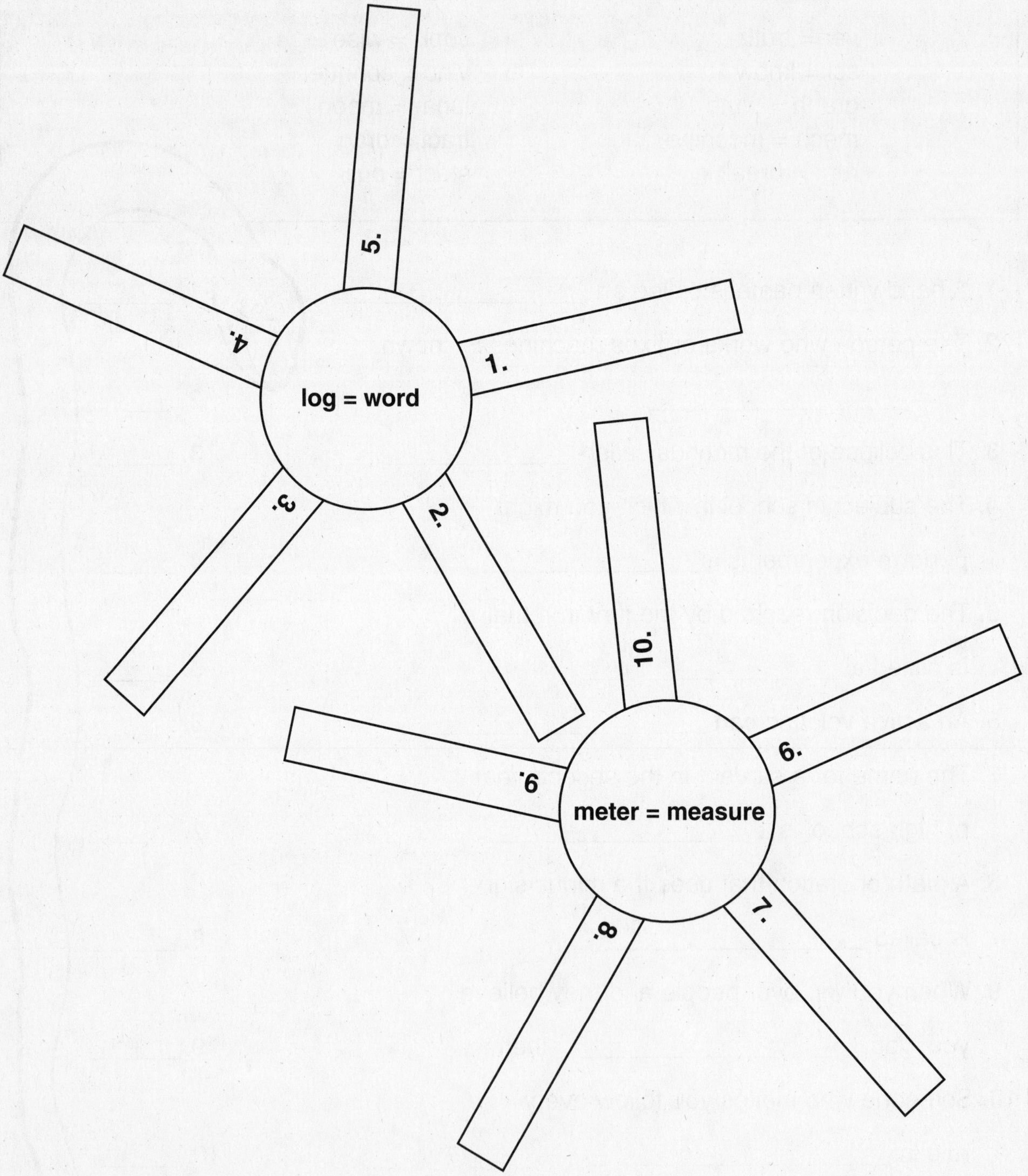

Using a Dictionary

The **pronunciation key** at the beginning of a **dictionary** explains how entry words are respelled. You can learn how to pronounce new words by reading the respelling. You also can find out how many syllables a word has and which syllable is said with more stress.

bi•an•nu•al (bī an´ ū ə le)

adjective happening two times a year

A. Write the answers to the questions.

1. What is the entry word in this dictionary sample?

____

2. What does the entry word mean?

____

3. How many syllables does the entry word have?

____

4. Which syllable in the entry word is said with an accent?

____

5. How is each syllable of the entry word respelled to show the correct pronunciation?

____

Go on

B. Look up the underlined word in each sentence in a dictionary. Write the respelling for the word, and circle the syllable that is pronounced with greater stress. Then write the word's meaning.

6. The opportunity to create unusual music is endless.

____

7. Where did that pianist receive her training?

____

8. Has any musician misinterpreted the composer's ideas?

____

9. The need for more violins was questionable.

____

10. Is it impossible to make music with spoons?

____

11. A quiet audience is not a sign of disrespect.

____

12. Please don't misquote the critic about the performance.

____

13. The thoroughness of the conductor amazed us.

____

14. The performance received a positive judgment from critics and audiences.

____

15. A performance of new music will occur bimonthly.

____

Name ______________________ Date ________________ **VOCABULARY**

Using a Thesaurus

A **thesaurus** is a writer's reference that provides synonyms for many common words. A thesaurus also includes definitions for the entry words and synonyms.

forgive *verb* give up feeling of anger or desire for punishment
▷ pardon to free from punishment
▷ excuse to overlook
▷ acquit to decide that someone is not guilty
ANTONYM **punish, blame**

A. Write the answers to the following questions.

1. What is the entry word in the thesaurus sample?

____

2. What new word is formed when the prefix *un-* and the suffix *-able* are added to the entry word?

____

3. How do the definitions of *pardon*, *excuse*, and *acquit* relate to each other?

____

4. How do the words *punish* and *blame* relate to the word *forgive*?

____

5. Write the new word that is formed when you add the prefix *in-* and the suffix *-able* to *excuse*. What does it mean?

____

Go on

B. Words with prefixes and suffixes are underlined in the explanation below. Use the thesaurus in this book to replace each underlined word with a word that has a similar meaning. Write the words on the lines below.

Our school librarian decided to (6) disregard his usual choice of realistic fiction. Instead, he read us a (7) remarkable but familiar fairy tale. The story was (8) incredible to hear again. It certainly was not (9) undeserving of its fame and popularity.

Some students thought it was (10) worthless to hear this story once again. Were these listeners (11) fearful of the strange, unknown events in these stories?

The librarian does not want to encourage any (12) misunderstandings. He believes fairy tales are for people of all ages. They are sometimes (13) helpful tales. They can also teach right from wrong, which is an (14) encouragement for people of all ages. These tales present lessons that (15) predate our times but apply well to all times.

6. ______________________ 11. ______________________

7. ______________________ 12. ______________________

8. ______________________ 13. ______________________

9. ______________________ 14. ______________________

10. ______________________ 15. ______________________

Vocabulary: Synonyms and Antonyms

Synonyms are words that have the same or almost the same meanings.

Antonyms are words that have opposite meanings.

Synonyms	**Antonyms**
delighted, happy, pleased	miserable, unhappy, distraught
rapid, nimble, swift	slow, deliberate, unhurried

A. Look at the underlined word in each sentence. Find the other word in each sentence that is a synonym or antonym. Write it on the line. Then write **S** for synonym or **A** for antonym to show how the two words are related.

1. This laboratory researches diseases and explores new medicines.

____

2. Did that spider climb the fence, then scale the building?

____

3. Please assemble the model, don't dismantle it.

____

4. I will pout or sulk if I please!

____

5. Do you despise these paintings and prefer those sculptures?

____

Go on

B. Write the words that best complete the paragraph on the lines. Then decide whether each word is the synonym or antonym of the word in **bold** type that precedes it. Write **S** or **A**.

warriors	treasure	soil	explanations	built
company	decays	gather	ignorant	rulers

6.-15. A farmer in China was digging in **earth**. Suddenly a piece of pottery appeared in the ______________. Little did this farmer know that he had found a **jewel** of ancient China. This piece of clay was part of buried ______________. Later, **thousands** of life-size clay soldiers and horses were discovered, but none of the wood chariots they were supposed to pull. Wood may **live** above ground, but it ______________ over time, especially when it is buried.

Why were these clay **soldiers** buried? It seems that these ______________ protected the dead **emperors**. In ancient China, buried ______________ had no **privacy**. They had the ______________ of clay armies and servants.

Today, people **flock** to museums and ______________ around ancient Chinese artifacts on display. Many are **made** of clay, while others are ______________ of bronze or jade. Are you **aware** or ______________ of ancient artifacts? There are many **questions** and only some ______________ about the artifacts of ancient China.

Writing Activity

Write a paragraph that explains something you know about the ancient world or ancient cultures. Use synonyms to avoid repetition and create exact descriptions.

Choosing a Tone

Synonyms are words that have the same or almost the same meanings.

think • ponder • meditate   careless • neglectful • reckless

Synonyms help create **mood**, or feeling, by affecting the **tone** of a sentence.

Ponder means "to weigh as you think."
Meditate means "to focus thoughts intensely."
Reckless has a more extreme meaning than *neglectful* or *careless.*

A. Write the answers.

1. If you are working hard to find a clue to a mystery, would you *look* or *investigate*? ______________________

2. You could describe something bigger than you as *gargantuan* or *grand.* Which word describes something out of the ordinary? ______________________

3. How would you respond to the best gift you have ever received in your life: *exhilarated* or *happy*? ______________________

4. A scientist tries to find the answer to why something happens. Which word best shows her effort: *working* or *toiling*? ______________________

5. Which word would you use to describe a person who experiences a swarm of bees: *harassed* or *bothered*? ______________________

Go on

B. Change the tone by choosing a synonym or antonym for each underlined word. Then revise the sentence. Use a thesaurus for help. Read one sentence and the revision aloud to a group and explain how the tone changed.

6. Elvis likes everything about music, especially guitars.

____

7. To Elvis, rock and roll guitar music is good.

____

8. He sees himself playing with a band onstage.

____

9. Just the smell of the wood on a guitar pleases him.

____

10. To play a song well, Elvis focuses on the guitar strings.

____

11. He touches the strings for quick, clear notes.

____

12. The sounds of the guitar and the electric piano meet.

____

13 & 14. Pleased people applaud when the song ends.

____

15. Back from his daydream, Elvis feels sad.

____

Writing Activity

Write a paragraph that tells about something you would like to be able to do. Underline some nouns, verbs, adjectives, or adverbs. Then rewrite the paragraph substituting synonyms that will change the tone and mood, or feeling. Read both paragraphs to a group of classmates. Which version do they prefer?

Word Attraction

Find a synonym (**S**) or antonym (**A**) for the underlined word in each sentence, and write each letter on a blank. Use a thesaurus if you need help.

1. **S** Would you like to sit on this seat? _ _ _ _ _
2. **A** Tomorrow is another kind of day. _ _ _ _ _ _ _ _ _
3. **S** Sid changed the story. _ _ _ _ _ _ _
4. **S** Afterward, they went bowling. _ _ _ _ _
5. **A** The group decided to extend its stay. _ _ _ _ _ _ _ _
6. **A** Farewell, my friend. _ _ _ _ _
7. **S** Permit me to be of assistance. _ _ _ _ _
8. **S** Never get into a fight. _ _ _ _ _
9. **A** The stadium is full tonight. _ _ _ _ _
10. **S** The dog is shaking because it's scared. _ _ _ _ _ _ _ _ _

The first letter in each word will answer the following question:
How do words attract one another?

_ _   _ _ _ _ _ _ _ _

Name ______________________ Date ________________ **VOCABULARY**

Alike or Different?

Use the clues to find the synonyms or antonyms in the puzzle. Write one-word answers on the lines. Then circle each word on the puzzle. Words may appear up and down or across.

S	N	A	B	R	E	Q	U	I	R	E	D
A	R	R	Z	L	Z	U	L	S	T	F	G
X	E	O	P	O	S	I	T	I	V	E	O
S	L	O	R	I	Z	E	Q	U	A	L	M
E	M	A	T	O	M	T	E	F	G	O	R
N	C	O	M	P	L	E	X	T	L	A	E
I	A	H	H	P	Y	S	A	O	L	E	Q
O	P	S	O	L	A	A	C	C	E	P	T
R	V	U	L	D	V	S	T	A	R	D	Y
I	M	J	I	R	E	V	E	R	S	E	K

1. anything but noisy ________________
2. not simple________________
3. very accurate ________________
4. late ________________
5. opposite ________________
6. not negative ________________
7. the same ________________
8. not junior ________________
9. if you don't refuse ________________
10. not needed ________________

Using a Dictionary

A **dictionary** is a book of words. It gives their spellings, meanings, and parts of speech. To help understand the meaning of a word, example sentences sometimes appear in a dictionary entry.

pillar (pil′ ər) *n.* a long, slender, upright structure used as a support for a roof. *As the pillar crumbled, the porch roof collapsed.* **2.** any person or thing thought of as like a pillar. *Our teachers are pillars of our education.*

A. Write the answers to the questions.

1. What is the entry word in this sample dictionary entry? ____________________

2. How many meanings does *pillar* have? ________________________________

3. Which meaning could apply to concepts such as *love*, *education*, or *democracy*? ____________________________

4. Which meaning applies to objects that are a part of structures or buildings?

____

5. What is the meaning of the word *pillar* in the following example sentence from the dictionary sample: *As the pillar crumbled, the porch roof collapsed*?

____

Go on

Name ______________________ Date ______________ **VOCABULARY**

B. Use a dictionary to look up the three words listed as possible answers. Then write the correct answer on the line.

6. a room where people relax

estate lounge portico ______________

7. the act of a child being born

experience delivery liability ______________

8. a step in a series; stage in the progress of something

degree estimate ascend ______________

9. a light for warning

fuse illuminate beacon ______________

10. the full range of anything

gamut vista embrace ______________

C. For each answer in Exercise **B**, make up your own sentence. Write the sentences on the lines.

11. ______________________________

____

12. ______________________________

____

13. ______________________________

____

14. ______________________________

____

15. ______________________________

____

Using a Thesaurus

A **thesaurus** is a writer's reference that provides synonyms—and sometimes antonyms—for many common words. Synonyms are words that mean the same or almost the same thing. Antonyms are words that

At the top of a thesaurus page, guide words show the first and last words to appear on the page. Also, a **cross-reference** word may appear in a thesaurus entry. It is another entry word related to the entry in which it appears.

absence/assemble

acceptance *n.* taking what is offered
▷ **agreement** fixing terms between people
▷ **approval** the feeling that something is good or worthwhile
▷ **embrace** the act of taking up in an eager way
ANTONYM: **rejection**. See also **setback**

A. Write the answers to the questions.

1. How do you know that *acceptance* is not the first entry word on this sample thesaurus page?

____

2. What synonyms could you substitute for *acceptance*?

____

3. What antonyms are listed in the sample thesaurus entry?

____

4. Why does "see also" appear before *setback* in this sample thesaurus entry?

____

____

5. How are *rejection* and setback related to *embrace*? ______________________

Go on

B. Rewrite each sentence. Use the thesaurus in this book to replace each underlined word with a more exact synonym.

6. For your health, exercise is <u>very</u> important. ______________________

7. At first, take it easy and don't <u>hurt</u> yourself. ______________________

8. Listening to music can help keep you <u>interested</u> as you exercise.

____

9. If you <u>like</u> team sports, join a team and practice regularly. ______________________

10. On the other hand, you can <u>walk</u> through your neighborhood.

____

11. You can <u>receive</u> information about an exercise program that's good for you from your school physical education teachers. ______________________

____

12. Don't be <u>shy</u> about learning a new sport like tennis or hockey.

____

13. You'll find that learning <u>new</u> skills will boost your confidence.

____

14. Even a <u>small</u> advance will make you healthier and happier.

____

15. Next thing you know, you'll be encouraging <u>classmates</u> to exercise, too.

____

Vocabulary: Word Choice and Connotations

Writers choose words carefully to paint word pictures for their audience and to create images. To do this, they need to know the differences among the meanings of words. All words have dictionary meanings. Some words also have shades of meaning, or **connotations**, in addition to their dictionary meanings.

What a flashy dress!

The dress doesn't flash like a light. *Flashy* has the connotation of "something colorful with an interesting design."

A. Choose the word within the parentheses that gives a more exact meaning for the sentence. Write the word on the line. Use a dictionary if you need help with definitions.

1. My, what a (small, minuscule) dog!

____

2. The grain of sand was too (small, minuscule) to be held in the tweezers.

____

3. The actor looked into the camera with a (wide, broad) smile.

____

4. My grandparents enjoy (ambling , moving) in the park for exercise.

____

5. A (group, fleet) of trucks cruised along the highway.

____

Go on

B. Replace each underlined word with a more exact word choice from the box. Use each word once.

delicious	robust	drift	splendid	fleeting

6. Did the kite go over the trees? ______________________

7. Winds make sailing nice. ______________________

8. In dreams, what seems to take a long time really happens in a short few seconds or minutes. ______________________

9. Fresh apples picked from my apple tree are good. ______________________

10. To play well in overtime, an athlete must be strong. ______________________

C. Find words to give the sentences exact meanings that paint vivid pictures. For help, use a thesaurus. Read your paragraph to a classmate.

Our pet St. Bernard, Wally, is so (11) ______________________, he can stand face to face with my (12) ______________________ brother. One day Wally found a hungry puppy that was very (13) ______________. We (14) ______________________ the puppy until it was healthy. Now Wally and Dina, the puppy, (15) ______________________ all day long.

Writing Activity

Write a paragraph that compares two places you have visited or two seasons of the year. Make your writing more exact and vivid by your word choices. Read your paragraph to a classmate or make an illustration.

Name ______________________ Date ______________ **VOCABULARY**

Similes and Metaphors

A **simile** is a comparison that shows how two things are alike using *like* or *as*:

She runs as fast as a cheetah.

The sun shines like a diamond in the sky.

A **metaphor** is a statement that compares two different things without using *like* or *as*.

My mind is a vast mural.

Clouds are pillows for dreamers.

A. Write the answers.

1. Write what the horse is compared to in this sentence.

My horse races like a lightning bolt. ______________________

____

2. What two things are being compared in this sentence:

The thunder sounded like a train wreck? ______________________

____

3. Does the following sentence contain a metaphor or a simile:

Stars are nighttime dancers? ______________________

____

4. What word signals a simile in this sentence:

The lotion was cold as ice? ______________________

____

5. Describe the cat in this metaphor:

The cat moves like a thief in the night. ______________________

____

Go on

B. Underline the things compared in each sentence. On the line, write *simile* or *metaphor*.

6. The grapes off the vine tasted sweet as butter. ______________

7. The horse's muzzle felt smooth like velvet. ______________

8. Happiness is a parade down main street! ______________

9. My room is my friend who shares my joy and my interests. ______________

10. Your voice sounds like gentle raindrops in spring. ______________

C. Complete each sentence with the comparison shown in parentheses.

11. (metaphor) Winter is

____.

12. (simile) My heart feels

____.

13. (simile) Receiving your letter is

____.

14. (metaphor) The song was

____.

15. (simile) The athlete was

____.

Writing Activity

Write a paragraph about a favorite activity or hobby. Use similes and metaphors to paint a picture of what it is like. Read your paragraph to a group of classmates and ask them to identify the similes and metaphors you used.

Name ______________________ Date ______________ **VOCABULARY**

Ladder Game

Play this game with two or more classmates. Take turns climbing down each step. To climb down a step, complete the line of the poem with a more exact word that paints a vivid picture. Read your completed poem to other groups. Try to be the first down the ladder!

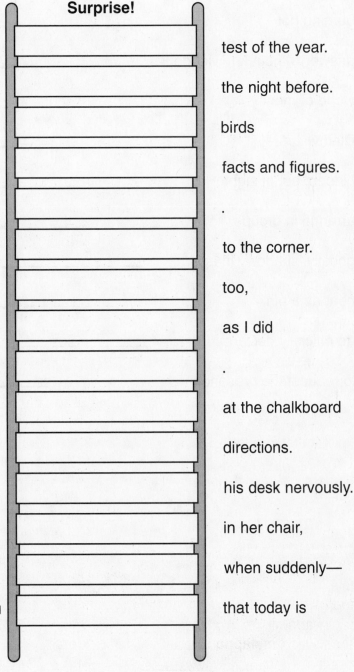

Surprise!

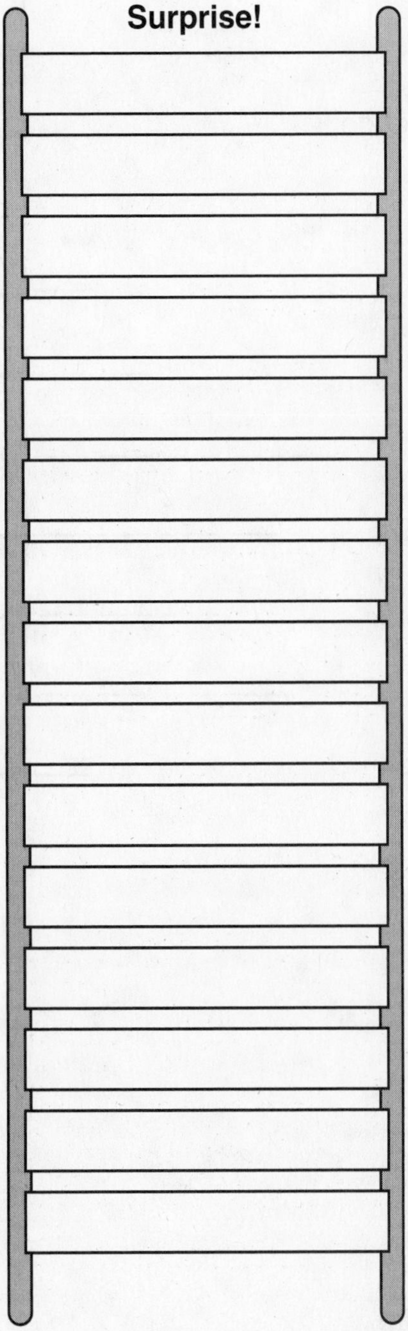

1. Today, I take the ______ test of the year.
2. For it, I studied ______ the night before.
3. My mind wandered like ______ birds
4. as I tried to ______ facts and figures.
5. By morning, I felt I was in a ______.
6. The bus seemed to ______ to the corner.
7. Everyone inside was ______ too,
8. because they felt as ______ as I did
9. from such a hard night's ______.
10. Now, I sit in my class and ______ at the chalkboard
11. filled with ______ directions.
12. Behind me, Joel ______ his desk nervously.
13. Adriana ______ in her chair,
14. hoping to disappear ______ when suddenly—
15. Our teacher says, didn't you ______ that today is April Fools' Day?

Word Choice Puzzle

Write the answer to each clue in the numbered boxes. The answers are words that fit the exact meanings of the clues. The row of boxes with dark outlines will tell you what the words you found show. You may use a thesaurus for help.

1. burning hot ___ ___ ___ ___ [ ] ___ ___ ___

2. answer without knowledge ___ ___ [ ] ___ ___

3. world of money [ ] ___ ___ ___ ___ ___ ___

4. filled with fire] ___ [ ] ___ ___ ___

5. hidden, out of sight ___ ___ [ ] ___ ___ ___ ___ ___ ___

6. arrange in groups ___ ___ ___ ___ ___ [ ] ___ ___

7. ghostly, shadowy image ___ ___ ___ ___ [ ] ___ ___

8. neat as a pin ___ ___ ___ [ ] ___ ___ ___ ___ ___ ___

9. to officially declare ___ ___ ___ ___ [ ] ___ ___ ___ ___

10. to request the presence ___ [ ] ___ ___ ___ ___

Using a Dictionary

Some words come from other languages or other historical periods. They may have interesting stories to tell us. Other words may have changed their meaning since first used. These **word histories** often are explained in a dictionary entry or as a special feature.

concise [kən sīs′] *adj.* expressed in few words; clear and short

Word History

Concise is a Latin word that means "to cut off." Writing that is *concise* cuts out words or sentences that are not needed to communicate an idea.

A. Write the answers to the questions.

1. What is the definition of the sample entry word?

____

2. What language does the entry word originally come from?

____

3. How can you tell when an entry word comes from another language or has a history?

____

____

4. What was the original meaning of the entry word?

____

5. How is the meaning of the entry word different from its historical meaning?

____

____

____

Name ______________________________ Date __________________ **VOCABULARY**

B. Look up the underlined word in each sentence in a large dictionary. Then use the language history for the word to answer the question. Write your answer on the line. (You may use more than one dictionary.)

6. The English word <u>language</u> comes from the Latin word for

____.

7. A <u>bandanna</u> comes from the word for "tying" in the

____ language.

8. <u>Purple</u> comes from the ancient Greek word for

____.

9. For the Gypsies of England, the word <u>pal</u> means

____.

10. The word <u>pronto</u>, which means "promptly," comes from the

____ language.

11. Ancient Romans used the word <u>companion</u> to describe a person they would

____.

12. The word <u>sonar</u> is a short form for

____.

13. The Old English word that our word <u>ship</u> comes from means "a hollowed-out tree trunk" because

____.

14. The word <u>parentheses</u> comes from a Greek word that means

____.

15. The word <u>Thursday</u> is named after Thor, the god of thunder and strength in

the ____ language.

Using a Thesaurus

A **thesaurus** is a writer's reference that provides synonyms—and sometimes antonyms—for many common words. A thesaurus entry shows the part of speech for a word and sometimes includes an example sentence. At the top of each thesaurus page are guide words that identify the first and last entry.

old/quiet
phantom *n.* ghostly or shadowy image
▷ **specter** a ghost or phantom
▷ **apparition** strange figure thought to be a ghost
▷ **ghost** pale form thought to be the spirit of a dead person

A. Write the answers to the following questions.

1. Would the entry word *quaint* appear on this sample thesaurus page? How do you know?

____

2. What part of speech are the synonyms for *phantom*? How do you know?

____

____

3. Which two synonyms are closest in meaning to *phantom*?

____

4. Which word would you use in a sentence to describe an image that is seen but not known to be a ghost or phantom for sure?

____

5. Why do you think example sentences don't appear in this entry?

____

B. Follow the directions to create a sample entry for a thesaurus. Write your answers on the lines below. Use the sample thesaurus from the previous page as a model and a dictionary or thesaurus for help.

6. Underline three words that are synonyms and circle one word that is an antonym for the entry word **establish**.

relate   institute   destroy   reject   found   install

7. Find the slash mark on line one. Write guide words between the slash mark that could appear on a page with the entry word *establish*.

8. On the next line, write the entry word and the part of speech next to it. Then write a definition for and a sentence with the entry word.

9. On the following lines, write three synonyms and their definitions. Then write a sentence with each synonym.

10. List an antonym.

____

▷ ____

____

____

▷ ____

____

____

▷ ____

____

____

____

Vocabulary: Figurative Language

A **simile** is a comparison that shows how two things are alike using *like* or *as*. *(A good friend is like a lucky star.)*

A **metaphor** is a statement that compares two different things without using *like* or *as*. *(A friend is a guiding light.)*

A **personification** occurs when an animal or an object is described as if it were human. *(When the wind screams through the streets, don't be frightened.)*

Onomatopoeia is the use of words that imitate or suggest sounds. *(If the buzz of a bee gets near you, stay calm.)*

A. Read each sentence. Write whether the sentence is an example of a simile, metaphor, personification, or onomatopoeia.

1. Did the water splash the wall?

____

2. Brad, I've always said that you are my sunshine.

____

3. Can you sing like a nightingale?

____

4. The water gurgles along the brook.

____

5. I'm a bit of a chicken when it comes to deep water.

____

Go on

B. Complete each sentence with the kind of figurative language shown in parenthesis.

6. Did you hear that small yellow bird?

________________________. (onomatopoeia)

7. The sound it made was as

________________________. (simile)

8. When I hike in the woods I am

________________________. (metaphor)

9. The tall trees

________________________. (personification)

10. The others catch up like

________________________. (simile)

11. In the wood stove, the fire

________________________. (onomatopoeia)

12. The brightest star

________________________. (personification)

13. Where else do people feel as free as

________________________. (simile)

14. Nature is

________________________. (metaphor)

15. How do you feel when the grass

________________________. (personification)

Writing Activity

Write the first paragraph of a story in which a character is lost. Describe the place where the character is lost and the character's thoughts and feelings. Use figurative language.

Onomatopoeia

Some English words come from other languages and cultures. Other English words that are **onomatopoetic** come directly from nature or experience because they imitate the sounds they describe.

Metal hitting metal makes the sound ***clang****.*

A rock dropped into water sounds like ***plop****.*

A cuckoo bird is named after the sound it makes: ***cuckoo****.*

A bell makes the sound ***ding dong****.*

A duck goes ***quack*** *and a cow goes* ***moo****.*

The horn of a car goes ***beep****.*

A. Identify the word in each sentence that is onomatopoetic. Write the word on the line.

1. There's nothing more frightening than the hiss of a snake.

____

2. For how long did the water drip?

____

3. The tic tock of the clock keeps me awake.

____

4. The geese honk as they fly overhead.

____

5. Did you hear the rustle of the falling leaves?

____

Go on

B. Writers use onomatopoetic words to make their sentences vivid and interesting. Use onomatopoetic words from the box to complete each sentence.

murmur	smack	splashed	neigh	moo
rustled	clang	squeal	clack	hoot

6. Alex wrote a story about an owl that would ______________ all night.

7. The owl lived in a barn with a cow that would go ______________ each morning.

8. The night owl would ______________ it's wings when it heard the cow, and then go to sleep.

9. One day, a farmer put a steel pail down with a ______________ on an iron plate.

10. Three ducks became frightened and began to ______________.

11. A horse backed into its stall and went ______________!

12. The owl woke from its morning sleep and ______________ its feathers.

13. Owls do not like to awaken during the day and hear a pig ______________.

14. Furthermore, the soft ______________ of human voices is something a night owl may not be accustomed to.

15. The owl wished to return to its dream in which it ______________ in the waves of the running river.

Writing Activity

Write a brief adventure story in which you use some onomatopoetic words. Read your story to the class and challenge classmates to identify the onomatopoetic words.

Poem in a Poem

Read the five lines of the poem. Then follow the instructions below. The words you underline will create another poem of five lines.

The Moon Rises Over the Forest

By day, the sun shone like a diamond in the sky.

We were walking along and humming.

By nightfall, the moon cried to be noticed:

"I am a fountain of delights!" We were left

quietly murmuring until we finally slept.

Follow the instructions below for each of the five lines of the poem above. Write the words you underline on lines 6-10 below.

Line 1. Underline the words in the simile that tells how "the sun shone." Write the words on line 6.

Line 2. Underline the word that is onomatopoetic. Write that word on line 7.

Line 3. Underline the three word phrases that is an example of personification. Write that phrase on line 8.

Line 4. Underline the sentence that contains a metaphor. Write that sentence on line 9.

Line 5. Underline the adverb along with the word that is onomatopoetic. Write those two words on line 10.

The Moon's Song

6. ______________________________

7. ______________________________

8. ______________________________

9. ______________________________

10. ______________________________

Go on

Crossword Puzzle

Complete the puzzle with answers to the clues.

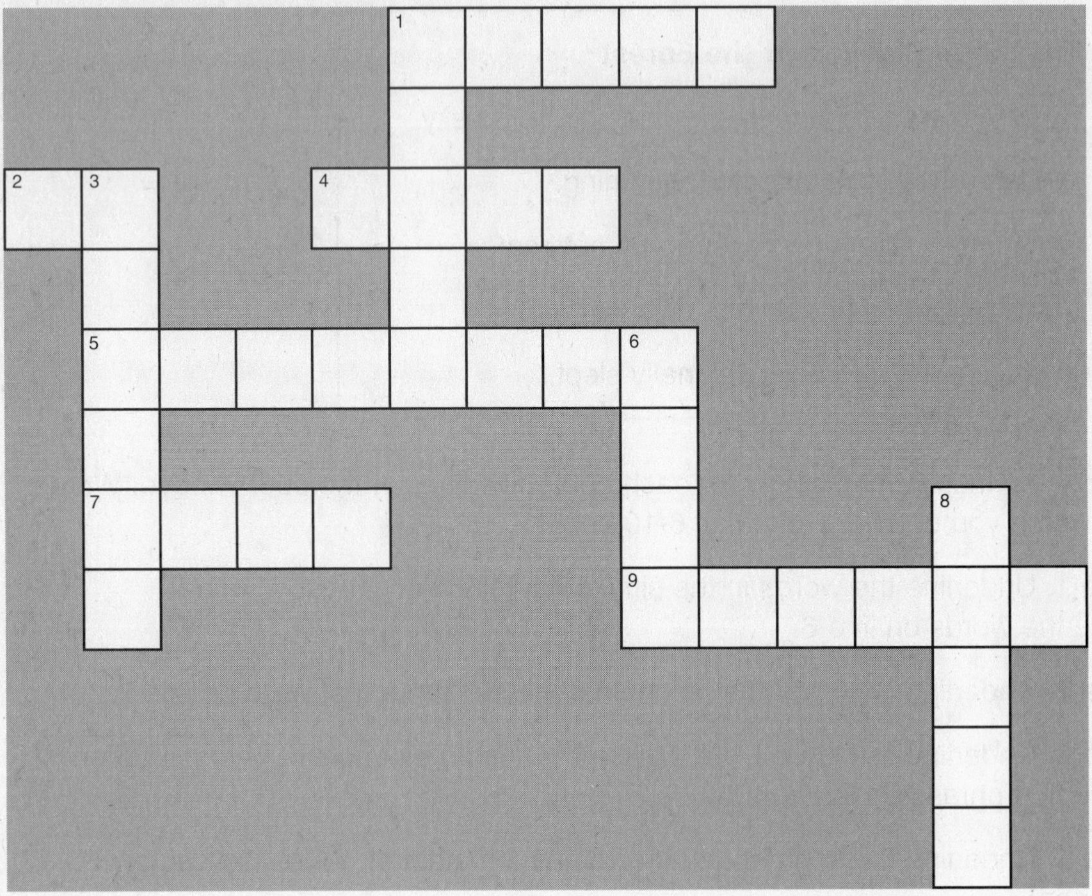

Clues

Down

1. sound of horse hooves
3. comparison with *like* or *as*
6. sound a lion makes
8. sound made by drinking through a straw

Across

1. sound of door hinge that needs oil
2. word clue to a simile in *strong as an ox*
4. sound of insects in flight
5. comparison without like or as
7. word clue to simile in a *smile like pure gold*
9. the sound of leaves blowing gently in a breeze

Using a Dictionary

A dictionary entry will usually show if a word has a homophone (words that sounds the same but have different spellings and meanings) or a homograph (words that are spelled the same but have different meanings).

lie[1] *v.* **1.** to stretch out flat **2.** to be in a flat position **3.** to say in the same condition *4.* to be located in a place **5.** to exist **6.** to be buried
lie[2] *n.* **1.** something said that is not true
v. **1.** to say what is not true **2.** to give an untrue idea

• Another word that sounds like *lie* is *lye*, which is a substance used to make soap

A. Write the answers to the questions.

1. How does the dictionary show that the two words are homographs?

____

2. Which entry only conveys an action? How do you know?

____

3. What homophone is given for *lie*?

____

4. What is an example sentence that could be used for the second meaning of **lie**[1]?

____

5. What is an example sentence that could be used for the first meaning of **lie**[2]?

____

Go on

Name ______________________ Date ______________ **VOCABULARY**

B. Use a dictionary to find the correct definition for the underlined word in each sentence.

6. My latest story is about a <u>pitcher</u> who throws fast balls.

____

7. When the crowds cheer her on, she takes a <u>bow</u>.

____

8. The <u>incense</u> she makes batters feel is legendary.

____

9. She rests to make sure her <u>forearm</u> stays strong.

____

10. When she starts to play, she rubs her <u>heel</u> in the dirt.

____

C. Complete each sentence. Use a dictionary.

11. - 12. What are two meanings for *meter*, which is a Greek root meaning "measure"?

____

____

13. - 14. What are two meanings for *firm*, which is a Latin root meaning "secure and fixed"?

____

____

15. What is a homophone that contains the Greek root *poli* that means "city"

____

Using a Thesaurus

A **thesaurus** is a writer's reference that provides synonyms—and sometimes antonyms—for many common words. Synonyms are words that mean the same of almost the same thing. Antonyms are words that have opposite meanings. A thesaurus also shows the part of speech for each entry word.

dismiss *v.* to send away; to tell to leave
▷ **discard** to get rid of; to throw away
▷ **fire** to send away from a job
▷ **discharge** to release from control
ANTONYM **retain, hire**

A. Write the answers.

1. What is the entry word and its definition in this thesaurus sample?

____

2. Which of the synonyms explains something about a job or position only?

____

3. Other than a job or position, from what could a person be *dismissed* or *discharged*?

____

4. Write a sentence using the verb *discard.*

____

5. What is an example sentence that would show how to use the word *fire*?

____

Go on

Name ______________________ Date ______________ **VOCABULARY**

B. One class made a thesaurus for words with Latin and Greek roots. For some entries, they need two more synonyms. Help by using your thesaurus to complete each entry with two more synonyms. Write each synonym and its definition on the lines.

rupture *v.* to break apart

6. ▷ ______________________

7. ▷ ______________________

benefactor *n.* person who gives money or help to someone else

8. ▷ ______________________

9. ▷ ______________________

pathos *n.* quality of an experience that makes you feel pity, sadness, or sympathy

10. ▷ ______________________

11. ▷ ______________________

fragile *adj.* easily broken, delicate

12. ▷ ______________________

13. ▷ ______________________

gradual *adj.* changes little by little or by slow degrees

14. ▷ ______________________

15. ▷ ______________________

What Is a Thesaurus?

A **thesaurus** is a reference source you can use to find synonyms, and sometimes antonyms, for many common words. **Synonyms** are words that mean the same or almost the same thing. **Antonyms** are words that have opposite meanings. Use a thesaurus when you are looking for a more interesting or more exact word. Read this sentence:

The sunset was pretty.

If you check the word pretty in the thesaurus, you will find these words: *attractive*, *beautiful*, and *gorgeous*. One of these words will make your sentence more interesting and precise.

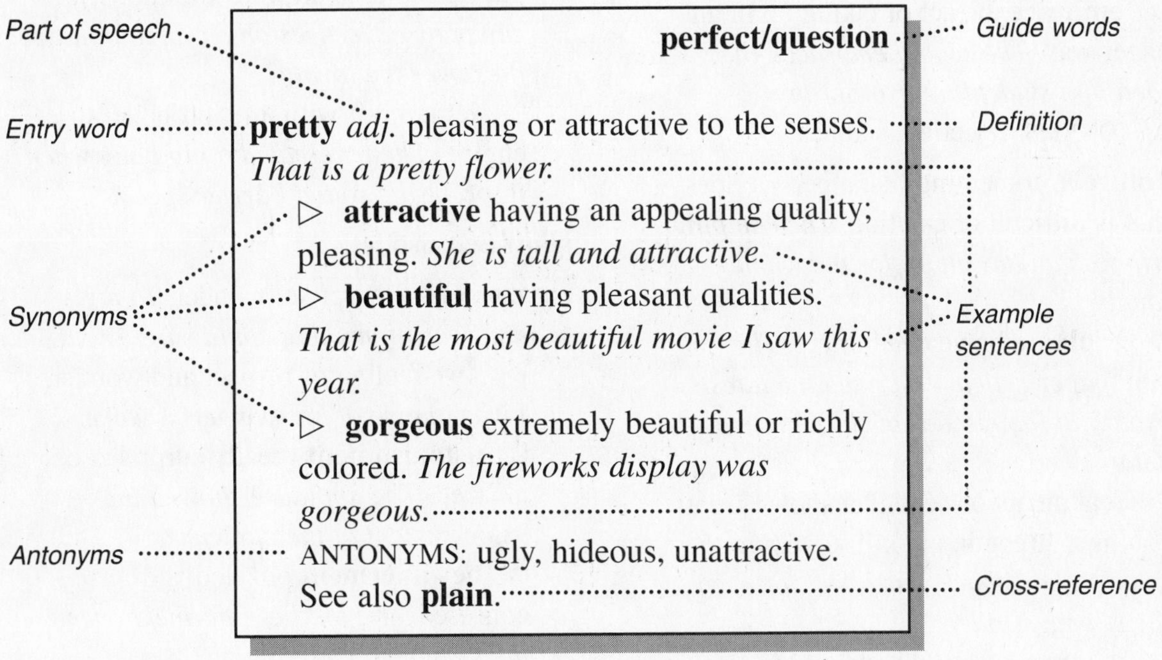
Part of speech
perfect/question
Guide words
Entry word
pretty adj. pleasing or attractive to the senses.
Definition
That is a pretty flower.
▷ attractive having an appealing quality; pleasing. She is tall and attractive.
Synonyms
▷ beautiful having pleasant qualities. That is the most beautiful movie I saw this year.
Example sentences
▷ gorgeous extremely beautiful or richly colored. The fireworks display was gorgeous.
Antonyms
ANTONYMS: ugly, hideous, unattractive.
See also plain.
Cross-reference

- The **guide words** at the top of each page show the first and last word on that page.
- The word *pretty* is the entry word.
- The **part of speech** of each entry is given.
- A **definition** tells what the entry word and each synonym mean.
- An **example sentence** helps you to use each entry word and each synonym.
- A **cross-reference** sends you to additional information.

A

acceptance *n.* taking what is offered. *With this acceptance, I will join the gymnastics team.*
▷ **agreement** fixing terms between people. *We signed our names to the agreement.*
▷ **approval** the feeling that something is good or worthwhile. *If I receive approval, I will become a tutor.*
▷ **embrace** the act of taking up in an eager way. *The school embraced the idea of a student tutor program.*
ANTONYMS: rejection, setback

adventure *n.* something that a person does that is difficult or exciting. *The camping trip was an adventure for the whole family.*
▷ **exploit** a brave deed or act. *The newspaper article described the latest exploit of the rescue squad in great detail.*
▷ **feat** an act or deed that shows great courage, strength, or skill. *Crossing the river on horseback was a feat for even the strongest rider.*
▷ **venture** a task or undertaking that involves risk or danger. *Taking part in a venture such as the search for a sunken ship needs great courage.*

after *adv.* a time following. *We went to the library after school.*
▷ **following** happening after. *The contest following the football throw is the toughest.*
▷ **later** coming after another time. *We will take a vacation later in the year.*
▷ **subsequently** coming later or after. *The mayor lost an election long ago, but subsequently got elected.*
ANTONYMS: See also **before**.

aircraft *n.* a machine that flies in the air. *That huge building holds many antique aircraft.*
▷ **airliner** a large airplane for passengers. *We met the passengers from the airliner at airport gate six.*
▷ **airship** an aircraft that is fueled by gas lighter than air, like a blimp. *The company advertises on an airship that flies over the town.*
▷ **jet** aircraft with a jet propeller or engine. *The jet created a big bang when it broke the sound barrier speed.*

allow See also **let.**

amazement *n.* surprise; wonder. *To my amazement, my dog could sing.*
▷ **awe** feeling of respect and wonder. *I was in awe of his wonderful voice.*
▷ **astonishment** greatly surprised or amazed. *The applause showed the astonishment of the audience.*
▷ **bewilderment** puzzled and confused. *We felt bewilderment over the unsigned letter.*

angry *adj.* feeling or showing anger. *Don's remark made me angry.*
▷ **enraged** filled with rage; angry beyond control. *The enraged lion growled loudly.*
▷ **furious** extremely angry. *Marty was furious when he found out I ruined his bike.*

answer *v.* to give a spoken or written response. *I wonder whether Celia is going to answer my letter.*

▷ **reply** to say in response. *If he insults you, don't reply. Just walk away.*
▷ **respond** to give an answer. *James did not respond to my question.*
ANTONYMS: See also **ask**.

appear *v.* to come into sight. *As soon as the first buds appear, she thinks it's spring.*
▷ **emerge** to come into view. *In the night sky, the moon was trying to emerge from behind the clouds.*
▷ **show** to be in sight, to be visible. *If you use thin cloth for the curtains, the light will show through them.*
ANTONYMS: disappear, vanish

argument *n.* a discussion of something by people who do not agree. *They had an argument about who was better at solving problems.*
▷ **conflict** a strong disagreement. *Sometimes a minor problem can lead to a more serious conflict.*
▷ **disagreement** a difference of opinion. *We resolved our disagreement by taking turns.*
▷ **fight** an angry disagreement. *Let's not fight over which movie to see.*
▷ **quarrel** an angry argument or disagreement. *The broken window set off a quarrel over who should get it fixed.*
ANTONYMS: agreement, accord, settlement, understanding

ascend *v.* to rise or move up. *The kite will ascend because of the wind.*
▷ **mount** to move up by climbing. *The cowhand will mount her horse.*
▷ **soar** to rise or fly up high in the air. *Some birds soar through valleys and canyons.*
▷ **sprout** to begin to rise up from earth. *The planted bean will sprout a new plant.*
ANTONYM: descend

ask *v.* to put a question to. *Let's ask for directions.*
▷ **inquire** to seek information by asking questions. *Please inquire at the desk.*
▷ **question** to try to get information (from someone). *Bill's mother questioned him about where he had been.*
ANTONYMS: See also **answer**.

awful *adj.* causing fear, dread, or awe. *The tree made an awful noise when it fell.*
▷ **dreadful** causing great fear. *I am in shock from the dreadful experience.*
▷ **terrible** causing terror or awe. *Jason received some terrible news.*

B

bandanna *n.* a large handkerchief often worn around the neck. *The bandanna had a red and white pattern.*
▷ **kerchief** a piece of cloth worn around the head or neck. *The kerchief kept my hair out of my eyes.*
▷ **neckerchief** a piece of cloth worn around the neck. *Ice cubes in the neckerchief kept me feeling cool in the heat.*
▷ **scarf** a piece of cloth worn on the head, neck, and shoulders for warmth. *Wear a scarf to keep your body heat from escaping from your head.*

beautiful
adj. very nice to look at

attractive	ideal
exquisite	lovely
fair	pleasing
good-looking	pretty
gorgeous	radiant
graceful	splendid
handsome	

ANTONYMS: ugly, beastly, terrible-looking

before *adv.* a time earlier. *Did you turn off the alarm before you got out of bed?*
▷ **formerly** at a time in the past. *Elizabeth was formerly known as Lizzie.*
▷ **previously** in time order, something before. *A vote was taken previously.*
▷ **sooner** ahead of time; early. *Summer will be here sooner than you think!*
ANTONYM: See also **after.**

benefactor *n.* a person who gives help or money to someone who needs it. *My benefactor paid for my ballet lessons.*
▷ **giver** a person who gives. *To be a giver, you have to be friendly and generous.*
▷ **patron** an important or rich person who supports people. *The pianist's patron arranged the concert.*
▷ **protector** a person who protects people. *The protector of these children make sure they get to school.*

big *adj.* of great size. *He works on a big farm.*
▷ **enormous** much greater than the usual size. *We saw an enormous elephant at the zoo.*
▷ **huge** extremely big. *That is a huge tree!*
▷ **large** of great size; big. *What large feet you have!*
ANTONYMS: See also **little.**

brave *adj.* willing to face danger; without fear. *The brave firefighter raced into the burning house.*
▷ **bold** showing courage; fearless. *The bold explorer walked into the dark jungle.*
▷ **courageous** having courage. *A courageous woman dove into the icy water to save the child.*
▷ **daring** willing to take risks. *The daring boy stood ready at the edge of the cliff.*
ANTONYMS: afraid, fearful

break *v.* to come apart; to separate into pieces. *These glass animals break easily.*
▷ **crack** to break without fully separating. *The shell cracked as the eggs were hatching.*
▷ **fracture** to break or split a bone. *Juan fractured his ankle and had to leave the game.*
▷ **shatter** to break suddenly into many pieces. *The vase will shatter if you drop it.*

bright *adj.* filled with light; shining. *Is that light bright enough to read by?*
▷ **brilliant** shining or sparkling with light. *The crown was decorated with brilliant gems.*
▷ **shiny** shining; bright. *Her blue coat has shiny silver buttons.*
ANTONYMS: dark, dull

broad *adj.* wide, clear, and open. *The broad avenue allowed everyone to enjoy a walk.*

▷ **comprehensive** something that covers all details. *The book was comprehensive when it came to grammar.*

▷ **expansive** covering a wide area. *The picnic area was expansive enough to hold the entire class.*

▷ **immense** very large and wide or vast. *He knows an immense number of riddles.*

ANTONYMS: narrow, conservative

build *v.* to put materials together to make something. *Can you build a model airplane?*

▷ **construct** to put materials together with a plan. *The family will construct a wooden sailboat this year.*

▷ **fabricate** to build something from materials. *He will fabricate a kite with paper, wooden sticks, glue, and string.*

▷ **manufacture** to make something in large amounts. *That factory manufactures cars and trucks.*

C

carefully *adv.* paying close attention to avoid danger or risk. *The tourists stayed carefully away from the edge of the cliff.*

▷ **cautiously** using care. *The bicyclist cautiously avoided the potholes.*

▷ **gingerly** with great delicacy or care. *Gingerly, I pulled the cactus spine from my thumb.*

▷ **warily** with care and caution. *The mouse warily poked its nose out of the cupboard in case the cat was near.*

ANTONYMS: carelessly, heedlessly, recklessly

careless *adj.* done without care. *The careless waiter spilled the soup.*

▷ **indiscreet** not careful about what one says or does. *The indiscreet thief left a glove with her fingerprints.*

▷ **neglectful** to fail to do what you should do. *The neglectful letter carrier forgot to tell us about the package.*

▷ **reckless** taking chances and not being careful. *The storm was reckless as it ripped through the field.*

ANTONYMS: thoughtful, prudent

chore *n.* something that has to be done regularly. *Setting the table is a chore I have to do every evening before I watch television.*

▷ **duty** an action or service assigned to someone. *It's my duty to check that the plants are watered every day.*

▷ **job** a specific piece of work. *The chart shows each student's job for the week.*

▷ **task** a piece of work to be done. *Cleaning the chalkboard is my favorite task.*

create
v. to bring into being

build	generate
compose	invent
design	originate
dream up	plan
fashion	produce
form	shape

ANTONYMS: destroy, copy

classmates *n.* people in a class together. *My classmates gave me a surprise birthday party.*

▷ **disciples** followers of a teacher. *The physicist is a disciple of Albert Einstein.*

▷ **scholars** those who learn through study. *Five art scholars wrote a book about the history of painting.*

▷ **students** people who study. *One group of students could not master the French language.*

ANTONYMS: expert, master, teacher

cold *adj.* having a low temperature. *There is cold water in the refrigerator.*

▷ **chilly** uncomfortably cool. *You need a sweater on a chilly night.*

▷ **icy** very cold. *You could see your breath in the icy room.*

ANTONYMS: See also **hot.**

concern *n.* something important to you. *My concern is that you learn how to play golf correctly.*

▷ **interest** wanting to know. *It was their interest that brought them to the mountain.*

▷ **upset** a worry. *The upset of a family was written about in the newspaper.*

▷ **problem** something difficult to be solved. *Her problem is that she can't swim on her back.*

concise. See also **short.**

cook *v.* to prepare food for eating, using heat. *Dad will cook dinner.*

▷ **bake** to cook in an oven. *Alice put the cake in the oven to bake.*

▷ **broil** to cook by exposing to a flame or another source of heat. *Let's broil the hamburgers on the grill.*

▷ **roast** cook with little moisture in the oven or over a fire. *Roast the turkey for six hours.*

cry *v.* to shed tears. *The sad movie made me cry.*

▷ **sob** to cry with short gasps. *The lost child sobbed until his parents found him.*

▷ **weep** to show grief, joy, or other strong emotions by crying. *The letter made Sofia weep with homesickness.*

ANTONYMS: See also **laugh.**

D

decay *v.* to rot; to lose strength and fall to pieces. *Food will not decay if it is kept frozen.*

▷ **decompose** to rot into individual ingredients. *Vultures find dead animals that are beginning to decompose.*

▷ **disintegrate** to break up into pieces and separate completely. *As iron disintegrates, rust forms.*

▷ **molder** to fall apart and rot slowly. *The skeletons of sea animals molder after they wash on shore.*

despise *v.* to strongly dislike. *I despise scary movies.*

▷ **condemn** to judge something or someone wrong or guilty. *Did the judge condemn the prisoner for life?*

▷ **disdain** to look down at with dislike. *The police disdain students who cross the street against the light.*

▷ **scorn** to feel that something is low and not worthy. *The referee showed scorn for the team's bad attitude.*

ANTONYMS: cherish, love, recommend

discussion *n.* the act of talking something over, often to exchange ideas.

▷ **chat** a friendly, informal talk. *Margarita chatted with her friends before the game.*

▷ **conversation** talk between two or more people. *They interrupted their conversation to give their tickets to the conductor.*

▷ **talk** an exchange of spoken words. *My uncle said he wanted to have a talk about our vacation plans.*

dismantle *v.* to take something apart. *Please dismantle the kite and store it in the closet.*

▷ **break** to divide into pieces. *Don't break the doll house into its separate rooms.*

▷ **disassemble** to take something apart. *You can build and dissemble this model car easily.*

▷ **raze** to destroy by tearing down. *A tornado can raze houses and barns.*

ANTONYMS: assemble, build, construct

dismiss *v.* to send away; to tell to leave. *Dismiss the class now!*

▷ **discard** to get rid of; to throw away. *They discard magazines they have already read.*

▷ **fire** to send away from a job. *The secretary was fired from his job.*

▷ **discharge** to release from control. *The fire chief discharged the firefighters from active duty.*

ANTONYMS: retain, hire

disregard *v.* to not pay attention to something. *Disregard the blue paint on one wall.*

▷ **ignore** to take no notice. *Did he ignore me or just not see me?*

▷ **neglect** not to do what you are supposed to do. *I promise not to neglect my chores this morning.*

▷ **omit** to leave out. *I will omit that statement from the record.*

do *v.* to carry out. *Some days I can't do anything right.*

▷ **execute** to complete; to put into effect. *The President's job is to execute laws.*

▷ **perform** to carry out to completion. *The acrobats will now perform a triple backflip.*

drag *v.* to move something along slowly or heavily. *The horse strained to drag the overloaded hay wagon.*

▷ **haul** to pull or move with effort. *It took three people to haul the file cabinet up the stairs.*

▷ **tow** to pull or drag behind. *I can hardly believe this little truck can tow an entire bus!*

drift *v.* to travel along without aim. *The leaves drift through the water.*

▷ **cruise** to travel along from place to place without great speed. *The ship will cruise from Florida to the Caribbean Islands.*

▷ **stream** to flow or move in a steady way. *The wind streams down the mountainside.*

▷ **wash** to drift because of the action of water. *A flood will wash the gravel in our drive away.*

dry *adj.* not wet; free of moisture. *Is the paint dry yet?*

▷ **arid** dry as a result of having little rainfall. *Nothing grows here because the land is so arid.*

▷ **parched** dried out by heat. *The drink felt good to my parched throat.*
ANTONYMS: See also **wet.**

dull *adj.* not interesting. *They walked out of the dull movie before it ended.*
▷ **boring** lacking in interest. *I almost fell asleep during the boring program.*
▷ **tedious** long and tiring, boring. *Checking all the addresses was a tedious task.*
▷ **tiresome** causing boredom or weariness. *Mrs. Rodriguez does not want to hear any more tiresome excuses.*
ANTONYMS: interesting, exciting, fascinating

E

easy *adj.* requiring little mental or physical effort; not difficult. *The math problems were so easy that Sheila finished them in five minutes.*
▷ **facile** not hard to do or achieve. *There is no facile solution to the problem of global warming.*
▷ **simple** not complicated. *The kit came with simple directions that were easy to follow.*
ANTONYMS: See also **hard.**

encouragement *n.* the giving of hope. *With my teacher's encouragement, the class wrote a wonderful story.*
▷ **assurance** words or acts that give hope and confidence. *With your assurance, I'll enter the race.*
▷ **motivation** the feeling to make one able to do something. *I need motivation to learn to play the piano.*
▷ **support** being carried or held up. *Because of your support, I will try even harder.*

endless *adj.* going on and on. *The rising temperature feels endless.*
▷ **boundless** having no limit. *The puppy's delight in play is boundless.*
▷ **continuous** going on without break. *This road is continuous from coast to coast.*
▷ **infinite** without a beginning or end. *He believes that space is infinite.*

establish *v.* to bring about. *Could you establish the rules of this game?*
▷ **found** to set up and support. *My friends I will found a new school club.*
▷ **install** to put into the proper place. *You should install new software on a new computer.*
▷ **institute** to bring into being. *The principal will institute a new dress code.*

explanation *n.* statement that tells what something is. *He asked for an explanation of algebra.*
▷ **clarification** to make something clear and easier to understand. *Could you give me a clarification of your opinion?*
▷ **definition** statement that tells what something means. *What is the definition of the word exegesis?*
▷ **justification** statement of fact that explains something. *The teacher asked the student for a justification of her opinion.*

explore *v.* to look through closely. *The class will begin to explore the history of space travel next week.*

▷ **investigate** to look into carefully in order to get information. *Each group will investigate a desert animal.*
▷ **research** to study carefully in order to find facts; investigate. *My sister did research about our family tree on the Internet.*
▷ **study** to try to learn about. *Next year, we will study geometry and world history.*

F

far *adj.* being a long way off; not near. *The farms are in the far regions of the country.*
▷ **distant** extremely far. *Many sailors went to sea to visit distant lands.*
▷ **remote** faraway, in an out-of-the-way place. *It took us three days to climb to the remote mountain village.*
ANTONYMS: near, close

fast *adj.* moving or done with speed. *A fast car can travel at 100 miles per hour.*
▷ **quick** done in a very short time. *She gave a quick response.*
▷ **rapid** with great speed, often in a continuing way. *Jeff kept walking at a rapid pace.*
▷ **swift** moving at great speed, often said of animals or people. *A swift runner warned the nearby villages.*
ANTONYM: slow

fasten *v.* to put two things together firmly. *We used a bolt to fasten the tire swing to the chain.*
▷ **attach** to connect one thing to another. *They used glue to attach the badges to our notebooks.*
▷ **bind** to tie or join together. *Our teacher will bind our stories into a class book.*
▷ **connect** to join together. *The driver connected the trailer to the truck.*
ANTONYMS: unfasten, detach, separate, disconnect

fearful *adj.* feeling or causing fear. *A howling wind makes me fearful.*
▷ **afraid** being frightened. *Are you afraid of dogs?*
▷ **anxious** worried and uneasy thoughts. *Swimming in ocean waves made him anxious.*
▷ **apprehensive** feeling uneasy or afraid about what may happen. *The child was apprehensive about her first day of school.*
ANTONYMS: bold, brave, courageous

finally *adj.* coming to an end. *The horse finally left the stall to run in the fields.*
▷ **conclusively** answers something definitely. *The evidence conclusively shows she is innocent.*
▷ **lastly** at the end of an order. *Lastly, I would like say I will miss this school when I graduate.*
▷ **ultimately** furthest away, most distant. *We would ultimately like to sail around the world.*
ANTONYMS: See also **first.**

fireplace *n.* place for a fire, often within a building. *Long ago, people cooked over an open fireplace.*
▷ **grate** metal bars for fireplace logs; fireplace. *We warned our hands over the grate.*
▷ **hearth** floor of a fireplace; life in a home with a fireplace. *His memories of hearth and home go hand in hand.*

▷ **wood** stove a kind of fireplace independent of the structure in which it is located. *The wood stove warmed the house during the winter.*

first *adj.* In time, before all others *Please take the first right after you pass the library.*
▷ **initial** of or at the beginning *The initial questions were easier than those at the end of the test.*
▷ **leading** out in front or guiding. *The leading horse found a good dirt path.*
▷ **primary** first in time order. *Our primary goal is to enjoy ourselves.*
ANTONYMS: See also **finally.**

flashy *adj.* See also **interesting.**

force *v.* to make someone do something. *Don't force Yuka to go if she doesn't want to.*
▷ **coerce** to make someone act in a given manner. *The bully tried to coerce the younger children to walk on the other side of the street.*
▷ **compel** to force. *The storm will compel us to cancel the game.*
▷ **require** to demand in a way that can't be refused. *The laws require drivers to stop at red lights.*

forgive *v.* to excuse someone for something they have done. *We forgive you for telling an awful joke.*
▷ **absolve** say someone is excused and not to blame. *Who can absolve a person who tells a lie?*
▷ **acquit** decide that a person is not guilty. *The jury will acquit the defendant because she is innocent.*
▷ **pardon** to excuse from more punishment. *The judge pardoned the prisoner, who then went home.*
ANTONYMS: punish, condemn

fragile *adj.* something easily damaged. *The glass vase is fragile.*
▷ **brittle** so hard it breaks easily. *The candy is brittle and crunchy.*
▷ **delicate** easily broken or damaged. *The delicate sculpture is held together with glue.*
▷ **weak** not strong. *When I am sick I feel weak, too.*
ANTONYMS: enduring, strong, tough

funny *adj.* causing laughter. *I heard a funny story on the radio.*
▷ **amusing** causing smiles of enjoyment or laughter. *Harriet found the monkeys amusing.*
▷ **comical** causing laughter through actions. *The baby made all kinds of comical faces.*
▷ **hilarious** very funny and usually noisy. *Hilarious laughter came from the party next door.*

G

gamut *n.* the full range. *The gamut of my hobbies goes from sewing to jogging.*
▷ **extent** an amount. *My coach can explain the extent of my training.*
▷ **spectrum** all the colors in the rainbow; from one end of something to another. *In the spectrum of colors, red is my favorite.*
▷ **sweep** the space or range covered. *There was a media sweep through town because of the election.*

gather *v.* to bring together in a group. *Gather the fallen apples, please.*
▷ **accumulate** to bring together in one place over a period of time. *When you accumulate 100 points, you earn a prize.*
▷ **amass** to bring together in one place as in a pile. *The recycle center is where we will amass collected newspaper.*
▷ **congregate** to bring together into a group. *The cows like to congregate in the meadow.*

gradual *adj.* something that happens little by little. *Learning to play a sport is a gradual process.*
▷ **continuous** going on but not stopping. *The continuous medicine cured the infection.*
▷ **piecemeal** piece or part at a time. *The house was built piecemeal over a full year.*
▷ **progressive** a series of steps that goes ahead. *Do you experience progressive improvement in your ability to write?*
ANTONYMS: sudden, instant

get *v.* to go for and return with. *Did you get the package at the post office?*
▷ **acquire** to come into possession of through effort. *How did she acquire so much money?*
▷ **obtain** to get as one's own, often with some difficulty. *First, you'll have to obtain a permit.*

gigantic
adj. very big and powerful, like a giant

colossal	monumental
enormous	mountainous
huge	towering
immense	tremendous
mammoth	vast

ANTONYMS: tiny, minute, microscopic

give *v.* to turn over possession or control of, to make a present of. *I want to give you this book.*
▷ **confer** to give as an honor. *The college will confer a degree upon the guest speaker.*
▷ **contribute** to give in common with others. *We are asking each person to contribute $10.*
▷ **grant** to give in response to a request. *Please grant me this favor.*
▷ **present** to give in a formal way. *Miss Kingsley presented a check for $5,000 to the Disaster Fund.*
ANTONYMS: See also **take.**

good *adj.* above average in quality. *He wanted a good meal.*
▷ **excellent** extremely good. *This is an excellent book.*
▷ **fair** somewhat good; slightly better than average. *He was a fair musician but a very good composer.*
▷ **fine** of high quality; very good. *Fine jewelry is usually very expensive.*
ANTONYMS: bad, poor

great *adj.* of unusual quality or ability. *Picasso was a great artist.*

▷ **remarkable** having unusual qualities. *The actors did a remarkable job.*
▷ **superb** of greater quality than most. *That was a superb dinner.*
ANTONYMS: terrible, awful
See also **good.**

grown-up *n.* some fully grown. *Do all grown-ups vote?*
▷ **adult** person, animal, or plant that is fully developed. *An adult elephant weighs tons.*
▷ **authority** one who has power to enforce rules or laws. *Who is the authority of these children?*
▷ **parent** mother or father of a person, animal, or plant. *The parent plant is taller than the young plant.*

H

happy *adj.* having, showing, or bringing pleasure. *Their visit made Mrs. Johnson very happy.*
▷ **glad** feeling or expressing joy or pleasure. *We are glad you were able to join us.*
▷ **joyful** very happy; filled with joy. *A wedding is a joyful occasion.*
▷ **merry** happy and cheerful. *Suzanne is such a merry person that she cheered me up right away.*
▷ **pleased** satisfied or content. *Was he pleased with his presents?*
ANTONYMS: See also **sad.**

hard *adj.* not easy to do or deal with. *These problems are hard.*
▷ **difficult** hard to do; requiring effort. *The hikers planned a difficult climb.*
▷ **tough** difficult to do, often in a physical sense. *We had a tough time pulling the boat out of the water.*
ANTONYMS: See also **easy.**

harmful *adj.* causing loss or pain. *Keep harmful substances away from the baby.*
▷ **destructive** causing or bringing injury or harm. *The destructive winds knocked down trees.*
▷ **hurtful** causing pain. *Hank apologized for the hurtful things he had said.*
ANTONYM: safe

heartbreak *n.* great unhappiness. *The heartbreak made him cry long and hard.*
▷ **anguish** great suffering. *She was in anguish until her stomach ache went away.*
▷ **grief** deep sorrow. *The family felt grief for its lost cat.*
▷ **mourning** the show of sorrow when someone dies. *The widow wore black as a sign of mourning.*
ANTONYMS: ecstasy, happiness, joy

headway *n.* forward motion. *The boat made headway toward the harbor.*
▷ **advancement** moving forward; making better. *The advancement of the hikers up the mountain was watched by park rangers.*
▷ **passage** act of passing or moving through. *We planned our passage from England to France by plane.*
▷ **progress** to go ahead. *Progress is the goal of our students.*

help *v.* to provide with support; to be of service to. *Mom will help me with my homework.*

▷ **aid** to give help to someone in trouble. *The Red Cross will aid flood victims.*
▷ **assist** to help, often in a cooperative way. *The whole class will assist with the project.*

helpful *adj.* giving help. *This book is helpful when it comes to sailing.*
▷ **beneficial** being of use or favorable. *A savings account is always beneficial for your future.*
▷ **important** having a lot of meaning or power. *Talent is more than important when you try to act.*
▷ **instrumental** helpful in serving as way to reach a goal. *Our coach was instrumental in our team's success.*

hidden *adj.* put or kept out of sight. *Sean searched to find the hidden image in the painting.*
▷ **concealed** kept out of sight. *Margo's fingers felt the concealed lock in the darkness.*
▷ **secret** known only to oneself or a few. *George finally found the papers in a secret drawer hidden in the desk.*
ANTONYMS: open, clear, obvious

high *adj.* located or extending a great distance above the ground. *The eagle nested on a high cliff.*
▷ **lofty** very high; of grand or inspiring height. *Above the valley rose a range of lofty mountain peaks.*
▷ **tall** having a height greater than average but with a relatively narrow width. *Over the years, the pine trees grew to be very tall.*
▷ **towering** of great or imposing height. *The city's towering buildings made Luis feel small.*
ANTONYMS: low, short

hoist *v.* to pull up. *The movers used a rope to hoist the piano into the van.*
▷ **lift** to move from a lower to a higher position. *Let's lift the lid, so we can see what's inside.*
▷ **raise** to put in a higher position. *Oliver raised the window to let some air into the room.*

howl
n. a loud, wailing cry

bellow	screech
shriek	wail
scream	yell
shout	yowl

ANTONYMS: whisper, murmur

hot *adj.* having a high temperature; having much heat. *This pan is hot.*
▷ **fiery** as hot as fire; burning. *Inside the volcano was a fiery pool of lava.*
▷ **scalding** hot enough to burn, often said of liquids. *I got a bad burn from the scalding water.*
▷ **scorching** hot enough to cause burning or drying. *The desert sun was scorching.*
▷ **torrid** extremely hot, often said of weather. *Much of Africa has a torrid climate.*
ANTONYMS: See also **cold.**

hurt *v.* to cause pain or damage. *I fell out of bed and hurt myself.*
▷ **harm** to do damage to. *An early frost will harm the crops.*

▷ **injure** to cause physical damage. *Warm up before you exercise, or you might injure yourself.*

I

identify *v.* to prove as something in particular. *Can you identify this flower for me?*
▷ **classify** to organize in groups by name. *The scientist will classify this unusual finding.*
▷ **name** word by which something is known. *I can name all the state capitals.*
▷ **pinpoint** to locate exactly. *I will pinpoint the bridge on this map.*

imagine *v.* to picture something in one's mind. *Imagine what it would be like to live in another time in history.*
▷ **guess** to form an opinion without having enough knowledge or facts to be sure. *Harold couldn't guess the number of jellybeans in the jar.*
▷ **suppose** to think about something as if it is possible or really happening. *Suppose that you had four oranges and Carly had two.*

impossible *adj.* cannot be done. *It is impossible to make gold from anything.*
▷ **hopeless** without hope. *My efforts to draw faces are hopeless.*
▷ **infeasible** cannot be done with things as they are. *Building a house in a day is infeasible.*
▷ **unattainable** cannot be achieved. *My goal to be President is not unattainable, but it is difficult.*

incredible. See also **remarkable, unbelievable.**

interest *v.* to cause curiosity. *Could I interest you in reading my new play?*
▷ **appeal** to find attractive. *The appeal of acting is becoming other people.*
▷ **inspire** to cause interest through influence. *After reading that poem, Tanisha was inspired to write one of her own.*
▷ **intrigue** to create interest through a fascination. *Hearing other languages spoken intrigues me.*
ANTONYMS: apathy, indifference

interesting *adj.* arousing or holding interest or attention. *Mr. Wu gave an interesting talk.*
▷ **captivating** capturing and holding the attention by beauty or excellence. *The tourists found the village a captivating place.*
▷ **fascinating** causing and holding the interest through a special quality or charm. *I just read a fascinating book about the space program.*
▷ **inspiring** having a rousing effect; arousing interest. *Her inspiring example gave courage to others.*
ANTONYMS: dull, boring.

J

journey *n.* a long trip. *We took a journey across the country.*
▷ **expedition** a long trip made for a specific reason. *The scientists will collect rocks on the expedition.*
▷ **excursion** a short trip made for a specific reason. *The bus left for the excursion to the zoo.*
▷ **trek** a long trip, especially when slow or difficult. *It seemed as if our trek would never end.*

▷ **trip** the act of going from one place to another. *The class will take a trip to the state park.*

judgment *n.* a decision. *Let the jury make a judgment about this case.*
▷ **discretion** an opinion or judgment. *You may go swimming at your parents' discretion.*
▷ **insight** a clear understanding. *With good insight, I decided on a trip to Italy.*
▷ **understanding** the ability to learn and judge. *With the coach's understanding, you may join the team.*

L

large See also **big.**

laugh *v.* to make the sounds and facial movements that show amusement. *They sang songs to make the baby laugh.*
▷ **chuckle** to laugh softly, especially to oneself. *Reading the comic strip made me chuckle.*
▷ **giggle** to laugh in a silly, high-pitched, or nervous way. *The two friends giggled over their joke.*
▷ **guffaw** to laugh loudly. *When Rick guffawed, everyone looked to see what was so funny.*

lawgiver *n.* a person who draws up a code of law for a people. *As a lawgiver, Thomas Jefferson wrote the Constitution for the United States of America.*
▷ **judge** person who decides matters. *Our case was decided by a judge.*
▷ **magistrate** person who can put laws into effect. *The magistrate asked the driver to pay the parking fine.*
▷ **referee** person who settles or decides matters. *The referee called the ball out of bounds.*

let *v.* to give permission. *Will Kyle let me borrow his bike?*
▷ **allow** to grant permission, usually in relation to rules. *Talking is not allowed in the library.*
▷ **permit** to allow to do something. *The club members decided to permit him to join.*
ANTONYMS: deny, refuse, forbid

like *v.* to take pleasure in (something); to feel affection for (someone). *They like cats.*
▷ **admire** to have affection and respect for (someone). *All the team members admire their coach.*
▷ **enjoy** to take pleasure in (something). *They enjoy playing chess together.*
▷ **love** to like (something) a lot; to feel great affection for (someone). *The children love that old mutt.*
ANTONYMS: dislike, hate

little *adj.* small in size; not big. *I have two large dogs and one little one.*
▷ **small** not large. *Violets are small flowers.*
▷ **tiny** extremely small. *A watch has many tiny parts.*
ANTONYMS: See also **big.**

look *v.* to see with one's eyes. *Look at what I found!*
▷ **glance** to look quickly. *The spy glanced over his shoulder to be sure he wasn't being followed.*
▷ **peer** to look closely. *We peered through the window of the shop.*

▷ **stare** to look at for a long time with eyes wide open. *Mac stared at the television during his favorite program.*

See also **see.**

loud *adj.* having a strong sound. *The band was playing loud music.*

▷ **deafening** loud enough to make one deaf. *The exciting goal brought deafening cheers from the fans.*

▷ **noisy** full of sounds, often unpleasant. *Their apartment is located above a noisy street.*

ANTONYMS: See also **quiet.**

lounge *n.* a room with furniture on which people rest comfortably. *We had a long conversation as we sat in the hotel lounge.*

▷ **lobby** waiting room or entry area. *Can you buy popcorn in the lobby of the movie theater?*

▷ **mezzanine** a story between the first and second story of a building, somewhat like a balcony. *On the mezzanine is a store where you can buy newspapers and magazine.*

▷ **parlor** a room where people sit and talk. *The board game was played in the parlor.*

lure *v.* to attract strongly. *We hoped the seeds on the floor would lure the gerbil from his hiding place.*

▷ **attract** to cause to come near. *If you don't want flies, don't leave out food that will attract them.*

▷ **draw** to cause to move toward, to attract. *The clowns make noise to draw a crowd.*

▷ **tempt** to appeal strongly to. *The offer of samples tempted customers into the store.*

ANTONYM: repel

M

manufacture *v.* to make or process something, especially using machinery.

▷ **assemble** to make something by putting the parts together. *Workers in the plant assemble cars.*

▷ **produce** to make or create something. *The workers produce a car every 20 minutes.*

many adj. consisting of a large number. *Jenna has many friends.*

▷ **numerous** a great many. *I have numerous chores to get done today.*

▷ **plenty (of)** enough, or more than enough, suggesting a large number. *There is plenty of food for lunch.*

▷ **several** more than a few but less than many. *Harold checked out several books from the library.*

ANTONYM: few

mastermind *n.* one who plans and directs. *Who was the mastermind of that April fool's joke?*

▷ **author** one who creates something original. *The author of that scheme was my sister.*

▷ **brains** the intelligence behind something. *The brains behind that movie understood many personalities.*

▷ **genius** powerful mind. *The person who invented the wheel was an ancient genius.*

mean *adj.* lacking in kindness or understanding. *Maya felt bad about being mean to her sister.*

▷ **nasty** resulting from hate. *The villain wore a nasty sneer.*

▷ **selfish** concerned only about oneself. *Pattie is so selfish that she never shares anything.*

▷ **spiteful** filled with ill feelings toward others. *It's best to leave Dan alone when he's feeling spiteful.*

ANTONYMS: See also **nice.**

meanwhile *adv.* the time between. *My father cooked dinner; meanwhile, I set the table.*

▷ **imminent** might take place but has not yet taken place. *Charlie knew that a new neighbor was imminent when he saw the empty apartment.*

▷ **meantime** the time between. *I wrote a story; meantime, Jennifer drew an illustration.*

▷ **pending** about to happen but not yet happening. *My dog will get a treat, pending my decision.*

mistake *n.* something that is not correctly done. *I corrected the mistake I made on the test.*

▷ **blunder** a careless or stupid mistake. *It was a serious blunder to forget the time of the game.*

▷ **error** something that is wrong. *The students found only one spelling error in their article.*

▷ **fault** a weakness or mistake. *The lack of light was a fault in the room's design.*

misunderstanding *n.* the failure to have an idea that is correct. *Our misunderstanding was about what time the party started.*

▷ **confusion** the failure to understand something correctly. *There was a confusion about what color to paint the mural.*

▷ **delusion** a false idea. *To think we were going to the movies was a delusion.*

▷ **error** to make a mistake. *An error was printed in the schedule.*

N

neat *adj.* clean and orderly. *Her homework is always very neat.*

▷ **tidy** neat and clean, often said of a place. *We raked the yard to make it look tidy.*

▷ **well-groomed** carefully dressed and groomed. *He is a well-groomed young man.*

ANTONYMS: messy, untidy, sloppy

new *adj.* having just come into being, use, or possession. *They are building a new house.*

▷ **fresh** new or seeming new and unaffected by time or use. *We put a fresh coat of paint on the old table.*

▷ **modern** having to do with the present time; up-to-date. *Technology is important in modern American life.*

▷ **recent** referring to a time just before the present. *Critics have praised her most recent book.*

ANTONYM: old

nice *adj.* agreeable or pleasing. *Her parents are extremely nice.*

▷ **gentle** mild and kindly in manner. *Grandpa's gentle words made Lisa feel much better.*
▷ **kind** gentle and friendly; good-hearted. *It is kind of you to offer to help.*
▷ **pleasant** agreeable; giving pleasure to. *Georgia and Scott are always such pleasant company.*
▷ **sweet** having or marked by agreeable or pleasing qualities. *He wrote a sweet thank-you note.*
ANTONYMS: See also **mean.**

now *adv.* at the present moment. *Please be quiet now!*
▷ **immediately** without a moment passing by. *When we heard the fire alarm, we immediately left the room.*
▷ **momentarily** for a brief time. *I spoke with him momentarily at the bus stop.*
▷ **today** the present day. *The class will go on a field trip today.*

O

obey *v.* to carry out wishes, orders, or instructions. *The dog obeyed and rolled over.*
▷ **comply** to act in agreement with a rule or request. *The people who comply with the order will be dismissed first.*
▷ **follow** to act according to wishes, orders, or instructions. *If you follow the directions, you'll do it right.*
ANTONYMS: ignore, defy, disobey

often *adv.* many times; again and again. *James is often late.*
▷ **frequently** happening again and again. *The two families get together frequently.*
▷ **regularly** happening at fixed times. *It is a good idea to exercise regularly.*
ANTONYMS: seldom, rarely

old *adj.* having lived or existed for a long time. *The old car broke down.*
▷ **aged** having grown old. *Our aged dog sleeps most of the time.*
▷ **ancient** of great age; very old; of times long past. *We visited the ruins of an ancient city.*
ANTONYM: young. See also **new.**

opposition *n.* condition of being against. *The person across the room from you is in opposition to you.*
▷ **contradiction** the opposite of something. *The facts in the case work together; they don't contradict each other.*
▷ **contrast** compare to show differences. *The contrast between the two colors makes each one stand out.*
▷ **reverse** to switch order. *Did the contestants perform in reverse order.*
ANTONYMS: support

outstanding *adj.* stands out. *The original Star Wars is an outstanding movie.*
▷ **distinguished** famous, stands out. *The distinguished artist signed autographs.*
▷ **famous** well-known, much talked about. *Are you the famous singer on this CD?*
▷ **notable** worth noticing or paying attention to. *Our mayor is also a notable public speaker.*
ANTONYMS: ordinary, commonplace, regular

P

pal *n.* informal expression for "a friend." *Jolene is my pal.*
▷ **acquaintance** someone you know with whom you share a common experience. *I had lunch with an acquaintance I met at the museum.*
▷ **companion** person who goes along with another person for company. *Will you be my companion on this field trip?*
▷ **friend** a person you know and like well. *Do you share your thoughts and feelings with your friends?*
ANTONYMS: adversary, enemy, foe

pathos *n.* the quality that makes people feel sympathy. *The pathos of the play had to do with facing hardship for the first time.*
▷ **emotion** feeling that is strong. *My emotions made me laugh and cry as I watched the play.*
▷ **passion** very strong feeling. *The passion of the author is felt through the writing.*
▷ **sentiment** tender feelings not based on reason. *The acting is poor, but the movie is a sentimental favorite.*

peer *v.* to look hard or closely so as to see something clearly. *I tried to peer through the grime on the window to see what was inside.*
▷ **gaze** to look long and attentively at. *They stopped to gaze at the toys displayed in the window.*
▷ **look** to use one's eyes to see. *Look at the pictures, and choose the one you like best.*
▷ **stare** to look very hard at. *Their aunt told them it was rude to stare at people.*

phantom *n.* ghostly or shadowy image. *In the shadows, a phantom appeared.*
▷ **specter** a ghost or phantom. *Did you see a specter inside the old house?*
▷ **apparition** strange figure thought to be a ghost. *Was that apparition of an ancient Egyptian?*
▷ **ghost** pale form thought to be the spirit of a dead person. *Do you believe in ghosts and goblins?*

plain *adj.* not distinguished from others in any way. *The meal was plain but hearty.*
▷ **common** average or standard; not distinguished. *Mumps is a common childhood illness.*
▷ **ordinary** plain; average; everyday. *Super Food is just an ordinary grocery store.*
ANTONYM: special. See also **unusual.**

pout *v.* to be unhappy and quiet. *The toddler would pout when no one played with her in the sandbox.*
▷ **brood** to think and worry. *The bankers brood about the stock market.*
▷ **mope** to be without spirit and unhappy. *With no one to play with, the child began to mope.*
▷ **sulk** to pout and feel apart from others. *Please don't sulk in a corner and not say a word.*

predate *v.* to date assigned earlier than the real date. *The check is predated for yesterday.*
▷ **antedate** to predate. *The law is antedated on the fifth, but it was announced on the seventh.*

▷ **backdate** to put a date earlier than the real one. *Even if I buy the house tomorrow, I will backdate the agreement for Monday.*
▷ **misdate** to give a date other than the real date. *Did I misdate my paper?*

pretty *adj.* pleasing or attractive to the senses. *That is a pretty flower.*
▷ **attractive** having an appealing quality; pleasing. *She is tall and attractive.*
▷ **beautiful** having pleasant qualities. *That is the most beautiful movie I have ever seen.*
▷ **gorgeous** extremely beautiful. *The fireworks display was gorgeous.*
ANTONYMS: ugly, hideous, unattractive.
See also **plain.**

Q

question *n.* something asked in order to learn. *The question was answered by the doctor.*
▷ **inquiry** investigation that helps to learn about something. *There was an inquiry about finding a new dance instructor.*
▷ **interrogation** the asking or examining of something. *The lawyer conducted an interrogation of a witness.*
▷ **query** the asking about something. *I have a query about a book I would like to have published.*
ANTONYMS: answer, explanation, response

quiet *adj.* with little or no noise. *The woods were quiet tonight.*
▷ **calm** free of excitement or strong feeling; quiet. *Sue remained calm as she waited to be rescued.*
▷ **peaceful** calm; undisturbed. *He spent a peaceful morning fishing.*
▷ **silent** completely quiet; without noise. *The room was silent while the principal spoke.*
▷ **still** without sound; silent. *The house was still and dark.*
ANTONYMS: loud, noisy

R

raise *v.* to pick up or move to a higher place. *Raise your hand if you have any questions.*
▷ **boost** to push or shove up. *Give me a boost, so I can reach the window ledge.*
▷ **heave** to lift, raise, pull, or throw, usually with effort. *The farm workers will heave the hay bales into the wagon.*
▷ **lift** to pick up. *Can they lift the table by themselves?*
ANTONYMS: lower, bring down, take down, drop

react *v.* to act as a response to something. *The joke made us react with laughter.*
▷ **counter** to oppose. *The children stood up counter to the teacher's instructions.*
▷ **rebut** show or prove that something is wrong. *She will rebut the charges by presenting facts to support her claim.*
▷ **retort** a smart, sharp answer. *That retort is an example of bad manners!*

ready *adj.* fit for use or action. *Is your costume ready?*

▷ **prepared** ready or fit for a particular purpose. *We were not prepared for our cousins' visit.*

▷ **set** ready or prepared to do something. *Everything was set for the picnic.*

really *adv.* in fact. *Was your dad really in the Olympics?*

▷ **actually** in fact; really. *Grandpa says he's 100 years old, but he's actually only 70.*

▷ **indeed** really; truly. *The person you met was indeed my sister.*

▷ **truly** in fact; really. *She was truly a great woman.*

receive *v.* to take or get. *I hope to receive a letter from my pen pal soon.*

▷ **accept** to take something that is given. *Our neighbor asked us to accept the gift with her thanks.*

▷ **acquire** to get or gain as one's own. *They hope to acquire more books for the library.*

▷ **get** to come to have or own. *That swimmer will get a ribbon at the end of the race.*

▷ **obtain** to get through effort. *They wrote to the director to obtain more information.*

ANTONYMS: give, discard, abandon, donate, distribute

remarkable *adj.* noticing because of being unusual. *The swimmer's remarkable strength helped her win.*

▷ **exceptional** standing out. *I can't stop singing that exceptional song.*

▷ **extraordinary** more than what is ordinary or expected. *Someone with an extraordinary voice can sing opera.*

▷ **incredible** impossible to believe because of being great. *Do you believe that incredible story about the haunted house?*

research *v.* to do a careful study of something. *The doctors will research the disease.*

▷ **examine** to look closely in order to learn or discover. *Let's examine what soil is made up of.*

▷ **investigate** to search or examine in order to learn facts. *The detective will investigate the crime scene.*

▷ **study** to learn. *I hope to one day study the ancient pyramids of Egypt.*

return *v.* to come or go back. *The visitor promised to return soon.*

▷ **recur** to happen or appear again. *The pain in your knee will recur if you don't rest the knee.*

▷ **revisit** to come to the same place again. *They plan to revisit the place where they first met.*

ANTONYMS: leave, depart, go away

right *adj.* free from error; true. *Her answers are always right.*

▷ **accurate** without errors or mistakes. *The witness gave an accurate description of the thief.*

▷ **correct** agreeing with fact or truth. *Is this the correct way to put it together?*

▷ **exact** very accurate; completely correct. *Get exact change for the bus.*

ANTONYMS: wrong, mistaken

road *n.* place made for cars. *This road is for automobiles only.*

▷ **highway** a direct and main road between places. *Do not go faster than the speed limit posted on this highway.*

▷ **route** to send by a certain road or set of roads. *Main Street to Elm Avenue is the quickest route.*

▷ **thoroughfare** a road or street open at both ends. *Along the thoroughfare people strolled or roller bladed.*

rude *adj.* not polite; ill-mannered. *Rude people never say "thank you."*

▷ **discourteous** without good manners. *It is discourteous to keep people waiting.*

▷ **impolite** not showing good manners. *Randy's impolite remarks made Mr. Parsons angry.*

ANTONYMS: polite, courteous

run *v.* to go quickly on foot. *Milo can run very fast.*

▷ **dash** to go very fast; to run with sudden speed. *Lou dashed to the telephone to report the accident.*

▷ **race** to run very fast; to run in competition with. *Sharon raced Mitch to the corner.*

▷ **scurry** to move hurriedly. *Mr. Flynn scurried about town to finish all of his errands.*

▷ **sprint** to run at top speed for a short distance. *Janet sprinted after the departing bus.*

rupture *v.* to break open. *The main water line ruptured and caused a flood.*

▷ **burst** to suddenly break open with force. *The balloon burst when the boy stuck a pin in it.*

▷ **fracture** to break or crack. *Did you fracture a bone in your toe?*

▷ **split** to break into two parts. *The ax split the log in two.*

S

sad *adj.* feeling or showing unhappiness or sorrow. *I know you're sad that they moved away.*

▷ **downcast** low in spirits; sad. *Ollie was downcast about the rain.*

▷ **miserable** extremely unhappy. *Peg was miserable until she made some friends in her new school.*

ANTONYMS: See also **happy.**

same *adj.* being just like something else in kind, quantity, or degree. *They both gave the same answer.*

▷ **alike** similar, showing a resemblance. *All three of the kittens look alike.*

▷ **equal** the same in size, amount, quality, or value. *Each child got an equal share of the cake.*

▷ **identical** the same in every detail. *The chair is identical to the one in the museum.*

ANTONYM: different

say *v.* to make known or express in words. *Candidates always say they will be fair and honest.*

▷ **declare** to make known publicly or formally. *The umpire declared that the game was canceled.*

▷ **pronounce** to say formally or officially that something is so. *The jury pronounced him guilty.*

▷ **speak** to express an idea, a fact, or a feeling. *Dr. García will speak to the class about health habits.*

▷ **state** to express or explain fully in words. *Mr. Jones stated his plan.*

▷ **talk** to express ideas or information by means of speech; to speak. *We often talk about sports.*

See also **tell.**

scale *v.* See also **ascend.**

scared *adj.* afraid; alarmed. *"I'm not scared of bats," he said.*
▷ **afraid** feeling fear, often in a continuing way or for a long time. *Nick is afraid to fly in a plane.*
▷ **fearful** filled with fear. *The child is fearful of strangers.*
▷ **frightened** scared suddenly or for a short time. *They were frightened until the storm ended.*
▷ **terrified** extremely scared; filled with terror. *I've always been terrified of dogs.*

see *v.* to receive information, impressions, etc., through the use of the eyes. *She could see the river from her window.*
▷ **observe** to notice. *Did you observe her leaving by the side door tonight?*
▷ **perceive** to become aware of through the sense of sight or other senses. *I perceive that you are unhappy.*
▷ **view** to see or look at, usually for some purpose. *Hundreds of people visited the gallery to view the artist's work.*

See also **look.**

short *adj.* a measurement not much from one end to the other. *It was a short time between snow storms.*
▷ **concise** telling a lot in a few words. *The speech was to the point and concise.*
▷ **fleeting** not lasting very long. *The rainbow was beautiful but fleeting.*
▷ **slight** small in amount or degree. *There was a slight difference in the plot of my story's final draft.*
ANTONYMS: See also **broad.**

shy *adj.* uncomfortable in the presence of others. *Van was too shy to ask Angie to dance.*
▷ **bashful** easily embarrassed; very shy. *Don't be bashful—come in!*
▷ **timid** showing a lack of courage; easily frightened. *Deer are timid animals.*
ANTONYM: bold

sick *adj.* having poor health. *Tom was sick, but now he is well.*
▷ **ill** not healthy; sick. *He was so ill that he could not eat.*
▷ **unwell** not feeling well. *You should lie down if you are unwell.*
ANTONYMS: well, healthy

small See also **little.**

smart *adj.* intelligent; bright; having learned much. *There are many smart students in her class.*
▷ **clever** mentally sharp; quick-witted. *He gave a clever answer.*
▷ **intelligent** able to learn, understand, and reason. *Dolphins seem to be intelligent animals.*
▷ **shrewd** clever or sharp in practical matters. *The woman's shrewd decisions have made her a success.*
▷ **wise** able to know or judge what is right, good, or true, often describing a person with good sense rather than one who knows a lot of facts. *In this folk tale, a boy is guided by a wise woman.*
ANTONYM: stupid

smile *v.* to show a smile, in a happy or friendly way. *Our neighbor smiled and waved.*
▷ **beam** to smile joyfully. *Dan beamed when he received the award.*

▷ **grin** to smile broadly with real happiness or amusement. *Walter grinned when he saw the picture.*
▷ **smirk** to smile in a silly or self-satisfied way. *Nina smirked foolishly.*
ANTONYMS: frown, scowl

soil *n.* the earth's top layer in which plants grow. *Dig a hole in the soil, then plant the seed.*
▷ **clay** sticky and stiff earth that is used for pottery. *Knead the clay until it is soft, then shape it.*
▷ **loam** soil with rotting plants in it. *The loam is like food for a young plant.*
▷ **silt** soil or sand that travel or that are left behind by water. *Silt helps to make the earth good for farming.*

sort *v.* to separate according to kind or size. *We need to sort the laundry by color.*
▷ **categorize** to group or classify things. *The librarian is categorizing the magazines by topic.*
▷ **classify** to arrange in groups. *We will classify the animals according to where they live.*
▷ **file** to put away in an arranged order. *His job was to file papers in alphabetical order.*

spacecraft *n.* anything designed to travel in outer space. *What was the first spacecraft ever launched?*
▷ **satellite** an object put into orbit around a heavenly body, like Earth. *Information from satellites helps us to predict weather.*
▷ **spaceship** vehicle that travels in outer space, usually powered by rockets. *The spaceship in this science fiction book is called Galactic II.*
▷ **space** shuttle a spacecraft that carries people and supplies between earth to space. *The space shuttle had a one week round trip.*

special
adj. different from others in a certain way; not ordinary.

choice	rare
distinguished	remarkable
exceptional	superior
noteworthy	uncommon
outstanding	unique

ANTONYMS: ordinary, common, usual, unremarkable

strange *adj.* differing from the usual or the ordinary. *We heard a strange noise in the basement.*
▷ **odd** not ordinary. *Jo has an odd pet.*
▷ **weird** strange or odd, in a frightening or mysterious way. *Kids say the weird house is haunted.*
See also **unusual.**

strong *adj.* having great strength or physical power. *It took four strong men to move the piano.*
▷ **muscular** having well-developed muscles; strong. *That shirt makes you look muscular.*
▷ **powerful** having great strength, influence, or authority. *Their new car hasa powerful engine.*
ANTONYM: weak

sure *adj.* firmly believing in something. *I'm sure I'll havea good time once I get there.*
▷ **certain** free from doubt; very sure. *Roy was certain he had left the key on the counter.*

▷ **confident** firmly trusting; sure of oneself or of another. *Wendy is confident of winning the prize.*
▷ **definite** positive or certain. *They have not made any definite plans.*
ANTONYMS: doubtful, unsure

surprised *adj.* feeling sudden wonder. *He was surprised at how cold it was outside.*
▷ **amazed** overwhelmed with wonder or surprise. *Daria was amazed to learn her father had once been in the circus.*
▷ **astonished** greatly surprised; shocked. *Everyone was astonished to see Mrs. Buford at the meeting.*
▷ **astounded** greatly surprised; stunned. *The judges were astounded by the gymnast's performance.*

T

take *v.* to get into one's hands or possession; to obtain. *May I take this book?*
▷ **grab** to take roughly or rudely. *Brian grabbed the phone and said, "What do you want?"*
▷ **seize** to take suddenly and by force. *The rebel army seized the tower.*
▷ **snatch** to take suddenly and quickly, often in secret. *He snatched the letter when she wasn't looking.*
ANTONYMS: See also **give.**

talk See also **say.**

tell *v.* to put or express in written or spoken words. *May I tell you an interesting story?*
▷ **announce** to state or make known publicly. *The principal will announce a new school program at the assembly.*
▷ **narrate** to tell about events, especially a story. *Mr. Bell will narrate Peter and the Wolf.*
▷ **relate** to tell or report events or details. *Each boy related his side of the argument.*
See also **say.**

think *v.* to have in mind as an opinion or attitude. *What do you think of our new math teacher?*
▷ **believe** to accept as true or real. *The police did not believe the man's story.*
▷ **consider** to regard; to believe. *We consider her one of the family.*

thorough *adj.* in every way complete. *We did a thorough search of the park for the lost dog.*
▷ **complete** without parts missing. *With this last piece the puzzle is complete.*
▷ **meticulous** very careful about every detail. *You did a meticulous cleaning of your room.*
▷ **total** a whole amount. *I saw a total eclipse of the moon.*

treasure *n.* something of value that is stored. *The treasure was buried in a trunk.*
▷ **fortune** a large sum of money that has been collected. *My entire fortune is in gold and silver.*
▷ **hoard** to secretly collect and store. *The extraordinary hoard dazzled the eye.*
▷ **riches** a great deal of money or wealth. *All the riches in the world cannot buy you happiness.*

U

unable *v.* not having the power to do something. *She was unable to read in the dark.*

▷ **inadequate** less than what is needed. *An inch of rain is inadequate for such dry fields.*

▷ **inept** foolish and wrong. *The clown was inept as he tried to run away from the elephant.*

ANTONYMS: able, competent, efficient

unbelievable *adj.* not to be believed. *The story about a singing giraffe is unbelievable!*

▷ **astounding** greatly surprised. *They applauded wildly after the astounding poem was read aloud.*

▷ **fabulous** difficult to believe. *We had a fabulous time taking the spelling bee because we knew all the words.*

▷ **incredible** impossible to believe because of being great. *Do you believe that incredible story about the haunted house?*

ANTONYMS: credible

undeserving *adj.* not ought to get. *The undeserving grade is due to a lack of study.*

▷ **meritless** not having good qualities. *The candidate was meritless when it came to experience.*

▷ **unwarranted** not having a good reason. *For a store to display ripped clothing is unwarrented.*

▷ **worthless** having no value. *I wouldn't buy the worthless merchandise in this terrible store!*

ANTONYM: important

unusual *adj.* not usual, common, or ordinary. *Jon writes unusual stories.*

▷ **extraordinary** very unusual; beyond the ordinary. *Monica is an artist of extraordinary talent.*

▷ **rare** seldom happening, seen, or found. *Some rare plants are protected by law.*

▷ **uncommon** rare or unusual. *Such a heavy rain is uncommon for July.*

See also **strange.**

upset *adj.* feeling uneasy; distressed. *Ben is upset about the math test.*

▷ **anxious** uneasy about or fearful of what may happen. *The family is anxious about Grandma's health.*

▷ **concerned** troubled or worried. *We are concerned about the flood.*

▷ **worried** uneasy or troubled about something. *Gene had a worried look on his face.*

ANTONYM: calm

useless *adj.* of no use. *The lamp is useless because it is too dim.*

▷ **futile** that does not succeed. *It was futile to try and do two things at one time.*

▷ **ineffectual** not able to bring about a desired result. *The loss was due to the mayor's ineffectual campaign.*

▷ **vain** with no result. *She tried to sew a new dress, but it was a vain attempt.*

V

very *adv.* to a great extent. *The basketball player was very tall.*

▷ **considerably** to a large or an important degree. *It will be considerably colder tomorrow.*

▷ **extremely** greatly or intensely. *May Ling is an extremely talented musician.*
▷ **somewhat** a little, to some extent. *We are somewhat tired today.*

vista *n.* a view in the distance. *The vista contained a valley with farms and a village.*
▷ **landscape** what can be seen outside. *We enjoyed the summer landscape from the mountain top.*
▷ **scene** a landscape. *My favorite scene is a winter storm with swirling snow everywhere.*
▷ **view** that which you can see. *How do you like the view from here?*

W

walk *v.* to move or travel on foot. *She takes the bus, but we walk.*
▷ **amble** to walk at a slow, easy pace. *There's nothing like an amble through the forest in spring time.*
▷ **hike** to take a long walk, usually in the countryside. *After the hike, we camped out in our ten.*
▷ **march** to walk with regular steps. *The band will march in the parade.*
▷ **stride** to walk with long steps, usually with a purpose. *Just stride right in, and tell him.*
▷ **stroll** to walk in a relaxed or leisurely manner. *Why don't we stroll around the block?*

want *v.* to have a desire or wish for. *Craig wanted to see you.*
▷ **desire** to have a strong wish for. *The group desired a leader.*
▷ **wish** to have a longing or strong need for. *I wish I were taller.*
▷ **yearn** to feel a strong and deep desire. *The boy yearned for rest.*

warrior *n.* a soldier. *The warriors defended their fort.*
▷ **combatant** a person who fights. *The combatants were stopped by their teacher and sent to the office.*
▷ **gladiator** a man who fought other men or animals for entertainment in ancient Rome. *The fighter was so strong, he could have been a gladiator.*
▷ **knight** a soldier in the Middle Ages who received this military rank of honor after serving the king. *The knight knew the rules of combat and followed them.*

wet *adj.* covered or soaked with water or another liquid. *Be careful—the floor is wet.*
▷ **damp** slightly wet. *The clothes in the dryer were still damp.*
▷ **moist** slightly wet; damp. *The grass was moist from the dew.*
▷ **sopping** extremely wet; dripping. *Linda took off her sopping shoes.*

whole *adj.* made up of the entire amount, quantity, or number. *How could you eat a whole melon?*
▷ **complete** having all its parts. *Make sure the kit is complete.*
▷ **entire** whole; having all its parts. *The entire week was rainy.*
▷ **total** whole, full, or entire; often referring to numbers. *The total bill was $14.27.*

worthless: See also **undeserving.**

Vocabulary Strategies

How many thousands of words do you know? Your **vocabulary** is made up of all the words you know, including their definitions. With a great vocabulary you're able to communicate exactly what you mean. A good vocabulary will also help you inderstand what you read. Use these strategies to build your vocabulary.

Context Clues

Often you can figure out the meaning of an unfamiliar word by looking at the words around it — that is, the word's **context**.

Word Parts

Many words can be divided into a beginning, middle, and end. Knowing the meaning of its **word parts** can help you to figure out what a word means.

Homophones and Homographs

Homophones are words that sound the same but have different meanings and different spellings.
Homographs are words that have the same spelling but mean different things.

Idioms

Idioms are sayings. They aren't supposed to be taken literally. Recognizing an idiom is the first step to figuring out what it means.

Etymology

Etymology means "the origins of a word." English is an amazing blend of words from other languages. Clues about a word's etymology can help you figure out its meaning.

A Dictionary

A **dictionary** is a reference book that lists words and gives their definitions.

A Thesaurus

A **thesaurus** is a reference book that lists synonyms. Any two words that have the same or similar meaning are synonyms. A thesaurus is a useful tool for finding just the right word for the meaning you are trying to express.

The Elements of a Dictionary

Guide words	Are the first and last words on the page. They help you to find the word you're looking for.
Entry word	Shows how a word is spelled. If the word is longer than one syllable, it's divided into syllables; dots are placed between syllables.
Pronunciation guide	Shows how a word is pronounced. Use the **pronunciation key**—there's usually one inside the dictionary's front and back covers—to see the specific sounds of each letter.
Part-of-speech label	Shows how the word can be used in a sentence, such as **n**. for noun, **v.** for verb, or **adj.** for adjective. Sometimes a word can be used as more than one part of speech.
Definitions	Shows the various meanings of a word. If there are more than one, the definitions are numbered, with the most widely used meaning listed first.
Example sentences	Show how the word can be used in a sentence.
Inflected forms	Show the plural form of nouns, the past and present participles of verbs, and the comparative and superlative forms of adjectives.
Etymology	Gives the origin and history of the word.

Pronunciation Key

Symbol	Sample Words
a	**a**t, b**a**d
ā	**a**pe, p**ai**n, d**ay**, br**ea**k
ä	f**a**ther, c**a**r, h**ea**rt
âr	c**are**, p**air**, b**ear**, th**eir**, wh**ere**
b	**b**at, a**b**ove, jo**b**
ch	**ch**in, su**ch**, ma**tch**
d	**d**ear, so**d**a, ba**d**
e	**e**nd, p**e**t, s**ai**d, h**ea**ven, fr**ie**nd
ē	**e**qual, m**e**, f**ee**t, t**ea**m, p**ie**ce, k**ey**
f	**f**ive, lea**f**, o**ff**, cou**gh**, ele**ph**ant
g	**g**ame, a**g**o, fo**g**, e**gg**
h	**h**at, a**h**ead
hw	**wh**ite, **wh**ether, **wh**ich
i	**i**t, b**i**g, **E**nglish, h**i**m
ī	**i**ce, f**i**ne, l**ie**, m**y**
îr	**ear**, d**eer**, h**ere**, p**ier**ce
j	**j**oke, en**j**oy, **g**em, pa**ge**, e**dge**
k	**k**ite, ba**k**ery, see**k**, ta**ck**, **c**at
l	**l**id, sai**l**or, fee**l**, ba**ll**, a**ll**ow
m	**m**an, fa**m**ily, drea**m**
n	**n**ot, fi**n**al, pa**n**, **kn**ife
ng	lo**ng**, si**ng**er, pi**n**k
o	**o**dd, h**o**t, w**a**tch

Symbol	Sample Words
ō	**o**ld, **oa**t, t**oe**, l**ow**
ô	c**o**ffee, **a**ll, t**augh**t, l**aw**, f**ough**t
ôr	**or**der, f**or**k, h**or**se, st**or**y, p**our**
oi	**oi**l, t**oy**
ou	**ou**t, n**ow**
p	**p**ail, re**p**air, soa**p**, ha**pp**y
r	**r**ide, pa**r**ent, mo**r**e, ma**rr**y
s	**s**it, pet**s**, **c**ent, pa**ss**
sh	**sh**oe, fi**sh**, mi**ss**ion, na**t**ion
t	**t**ag, fa**t**, bu**tt**on, dresse**d**
th	**th**in, pan**th**er, bo**th**
$\underline{\text{th}}$	**th**is, mo**th**er, smoo**th**
u	**u**p, m**u**d, l**o**ve, d**ou**ble
ū	**u**se, m**u**le, c**ue**, f**eu**d, f**ew**
ü	r**u**le, tr**ue**, f**oo**d
u̇	p**u**t, w**ou**ld, sh**ou**ld
ûr	b**ur**n, t**er**m, w**or**d, c**our**age
v	**v**ery, fa**v**or, wa**v**e
w	**w**et, **w**eather, re**w**ard
y	**y**es, on**i**on
z	**z**oo, ja**zz**, ro**s**e, dog**s**, hou**s**es
zh	vi**s**ion, trea**s**ure, a**z**ure
ə	**a**bout, tak**e**n, penc**i**l, lem**o**n, circ**u**s

My Word List